D0472348

LANCASTER BAPTIST CHURCH

*Twenty-Five Years of*

# CORRESPONDENCE

*Letters Received from Pastors and*

*Friends over the Years*

COMPILED BY

# PAUL W. CHAPPELL

Copyright © 2011 by Striving Together Publications.
All Scripture quotations are taken from the King James Version.

First published in 2011 by Striving Together Publications, a ministry of Lancaster Baptist Church, Lancaster, CA 93535. Striving Together Publications is committed to providing tried, trusted, and proven resources that will further equip local churches to carry out the Great Commission. Your comments and suggestions are valued.

All rights reserved. No part of this book may be reproduced, stored in a retrieval system, or transmitted in any form or by any means—electronic, mechanical, photocopy, recording, or otherwise—without written permission of the publisher, except for brief quotations in printed reviews.

Striving Together Publications
4020 E. Lancaster Blvd.
Lancaster, CA 93535
800.201.7748

Cover design by Andrew Jones
Layout by Craig Parker
Special thanks to our proofreaders

Letters are used by permission from their authors.

ISBN 978-1-59894-172-2

**Printed in the United States of America**

# Table of Contents

# Special Thanks

I would like to thank...

Mrs. Bonnie Ferrso for her faithfulness as my secretary over the last twenty years and her expertise in many areas, including filing my correspondence.

Monica Bass for helping me compile this collection.

The Lancaster Baptist Church Family for making and sharing the twenty-five years of memories reflected upon in these letters.

# Preface

Over the journey of our lives, there are markers along the trail that remind us of where we have been and where we are going. The twelve drawers of letter files in my office hold many such markers for me. Over the past few months, in anticipation of our church's twenty-fifth anniversary, I've taken some time to read through many of these letters.

The hours I spent over these treasured pages were both educational and inspirational. I compiled a sampling of them for our church and friends of our ministry, and I believe they will be encouraging and edifying to you. This collection is produced to show the wonderful support that exists among Bible-believing pastors and the love and encouragement we give to one another. I am extremely grateful for the help I've received from my brethren over the years. They have helped me bear the burdens with more grace.

As a whole, these letters provide four unique perspectives:

**Historical**—As I traveled down memory lane with these letters, I was reminded anew of our rich heritage as independent Baptists. Many of the letters were written from the pens of giants of the faith, some of whom are now with the Lord. These letters are a link to the past—a glimpse into the hearts of men who walked with God and led our movement in "the old days." I noted that the themes of their letters were similar, and they centered on soulwinning, personal purity, biblical preaching, and a willingness to stand for truth. It is my desire to continue—and share with you—their emphasis as we reach our world with the Gospel.

**Inspirational**—Over the past twenty-five years, our church has seen incredible victories—God's miraculous hand of blessing. Many of these letters refer to some of our sweetest victories, and they offer a unique perspective from the "outside" of what God has done here. They cause me to rejoice in the blessings of the past and to yearn for more of God's blessing in the future. They inspire me to continue to walk the old paths and keep soulwinning and discipleship at the heart of our ministry.

**Educational**—Some of these letters contain a wealth of treasured advice from men who have mentored me in life and ministry. From the letter Dr. Jack Baskin wrote me—a sixteen-year-old missionary kid—encouraging me to submit my strong will to God, to the letter Dr. Eldon Martens wrote me just hours before he went to be with the

Lord, I'm deeply thankful for the investment men of God have made in my life. I'd like to pass on some of their wisdom to you.

**Relational**—The longer I serve the Lord, the more precious friendship and fellowship becomes. I'm thankful for encouraging friends who, through both example and word, have strengthened and sharpened me in the ministry. Their letters are a reminder to me of the power of encouragement and the value of relationships. I'm thankful that I get to strive together for the faith with so many in this generation who love God supremely and serve Him wholeheartedly.

I pray this collection is the help to you that it was to me. I hope you enjoy reading these signposts of the past and that through these pages, you, like me, will be fueled with vision for the future.

PART 1

# 25ᵀᴴ ANNIVERSARY LETTERS

# PASTORS A–I

# GREATER PORTLAND
## BAPTIST GPBC CHURCH

Home of
Greater Portland
Christian Academy

Dr. Rick Adams,
Sr. Pastor

Assistant Pastors:

Dr. Greg Adams
Rev. Brad McFeters,
Rev. Bob Boyd, Jr.

17800
SE Main St.

Portland, OR
97233

Phone
503.761.1136

FAX
503.761.6971

www.gpbcweb.org

May 10, 2011

Pastor Paul Chappell
Lancaster Baptist Church
4020 E Lancaster Blvd
Lancaster, CA 93535

Dear Brother Chappell,

This is just a note to congratulate you and Terry on celebrating your 25 years of ministry there at Lancaster Baptist Church. I remember when the Lord called you to go to Lancaster, and for the last 25 years I have watched with much admiration and rejoicing in every victory that God has given you. It has been my privilege to preach with and for you through those years and I have been humbled not only by your kindness and generosity but also have been blessed by your wisdom and your faithful counsel and encouragement.

Thank you always seems inadequate, perhaps I love you says it best. I wish you, your staff, and of course your family a wonderful time of celebration. While I am unable to be there to personally celebrate with you, please know that every victory and every triumph that God has given you is an answer to prayer from a friend.

Rest assured of my friendship. If I can ever be of assistance to you, feel free to call at any time. Until then, I will be...

Ever Your Friend in Christ,

Dr. Rick Adams, Pastor

RTA/efd

Follow your heart home to GPBC!

9

KEVIN ALBERT, *Pastor*
TONY BROWN, *Music Ministry*
STEVE VON BOKERN, *Student Ministries*
JOHN WINDERS, *Bus Ministry*

February 3, 2011

Dear Pastor Chappell,

I am writing to congratulate you on the twenty-five years of faithful and fruitful ministry at the Lancaster Baptist Church. Your example has been an inspiration to me and many other pastors. You have embodied the spirit of "grace and truth" that our Saviour was full of as He ministered in this world.

I appreciate so much the individual time that you have invested in my children and the other students from our church. Thank you for caring about them and sharing your life with them. Your labour has not been in vain, but will last for all eternity. May the Lord bless you with many more years of fruitful service for Him.

Your Friend,

Kevin Albert

Kevin Albert

**GRACE BAPTIST CHURCH**

*Jeffrey Amsbaugh*
SENIOR PASTOR

*Greg Powell*
ASSOCIATE PASTOR

*Bert Arrowood*
ASSISTANT PASTOR

*Mark Liedtke*
SPANISH PASTOR

*January 28, 2011*

**Dear Pastor Chappell,**

*Several years ago at the advice of Dr. Sisk, I made my first trip to Lancaster Baptist Church and West Coast Baptist College. To some degree, I felt like the queen of Sheba - the half had not been told me.*

*From the very first time that I walked on the campus, it was clear that there was an evident love for the souls of men and a given hospitality to the saints of God. Karen and I were immediately impressed and began to make arrangements for our oldest daughter Ashley to further her education. During the time that she has been under your tutelage and experienced your preaching, God has done a marvelous work in her life as she prepares, Lord willing, to serve Him on the mission field one day. Words cannot begin to describe the joy that we feel in the way that God has used your wonderful ministry to impact the life of our child.*

*Your friendship has been dear and precious as we have served on boards and on platforms together, and your staff has been a tremendous help to me during the time that we have been acquainted.*

*On this wonderful milestone of celebrating your 25 years of ministry, I want to congratulate you and thank you for all the impact that you have made in the life of this preacher and numerous others across our land.*

*May God continue to use you as you reach the next generation of fundamentalists with the gospel of Jesus Christ.*

*God's best,*

**Jeff Amsbaugh**

*Experience a Touch of Grace*

2915 FOURTEENTH AVENUE • COLUMBUS, GEORGIA 31904 • 706-323-1046 • FAX 706-323-8554

WWW.AMAZINGGRACE.NET

**Tucson**
BAPTIST TEMPLE

Jan 11

Pastor Chappell—

Congrats on reaching such a significant milestone in your ministry. Thank you for 25 years of faithfulness. Your faithful preaching, loving, counseling, soulwinning, teaching, writing, and example have changed my life forever. You are a modern day "Paul" in so many ways.

May God grant you many more years to serve Him!

Privileged to be your friend—

Brent D Armstrong
*Pastor*

Brent
Phili:%-21

12

# Victory Baptist Church

March 4, 2011

Pastor Paul Chappell
Lancaster Baptist Church
4020 E. Lancaster Blvd.
Lancaster, CA 91601

Dear Pastor Chappell,

Greetings from Burbank, California! I pray that this letter finds you well and enjoying a tremendous year of blessing as you continue to serve our Lord Jesus Christ.

I wish to extend to you and to your family my warmest and most heartfelt congratulations for achieving 25 years of faithful and fruitful ministry at Lancaster Baptist Church! Our family first arrived at Lancaster Baptist to prepare for ministry at West Coast during the summer of your 15th anniversary. I clearly remember the overwhelming feeling in my heart that God was doing something extraordinary in the church and through your leadership. And for the next four years you poured your heart and soul into ours – shaping and molding us into ready servants of Jesus Christ. Those were some of the best years of my life!

Pastor, thank you for "staying by the stuff" for 25 years! I am certain that it was not easy. I know that there have been difficult days and long nights, but by staying faithful you have impacted this young man's life in ways you will never know. Thank you for beginning West Coast Baptist College. We learned soulwinning, discipleship, hospitality, faithful preaching, and diligent mentorship by watching your example and through the lessons that we learned in the classroom. Thank you for keeping Christ first, your family a priority, and service to God fundamental. Thank you for teaching me to keep the main thing the main thing! Thank you for never giving up and for being a leader worthy of following. I cannot imagine the price that you have paid to provide your life as an example, but thank you for counting the cost and finding it worthy of sacrifice.

Thank you for providing to fundamentalism balance and grace. You have taught us how to be a servant leader – faithful to the ancient truths of God's Word while lovingly nurturing young believers in the faith. You have showed us how to dream of future blessings unseen over the horizon while being solidly anchored to our treasured past. I have watched you invest at great cost and sacrifice, without measure and obligation, into the lives of those who both love and despise you. In this you have taught me the greatest lesson of life – unconditional love. In this also, you have shown me Christ Himself.

I love you, Pastor, and I rejoice in all that God has done. I carry in my heart much of what you are, and in so many ways, I am most proud of that. You have been a spiritual father, friend, and co-laborer and I pray, a faithful companion to the end! Press on, Pastor, and in pressing on we go forward together. Congratulations on 25 years of ministry – I look forward to 25 more!

Love in Christ,

Rob Badger
Pastor

*experience victory in Jesus*

3440 W. Alameda Ave. | Burbank, CA 91505 | 818.915.4825
www.vbcnorthhollywood.org | Rob Badger, Pastor

13

*From the Office of*

## Dr. Raymond W. Barber

621 Curtis Road
Burleson, Texas 76028
E-Mail: Raymond.Barber@att.net · 817-295-2829

January 27, 2011

Dr. Paul Chappell
Lancaster Baptist Church
4020 E. Lancaster Boulevard
Lancaster, CA 93535

Dear Paul:

Congratulations upon the celebration of your *twenty-five years of ministry* at Lancaster Baptist Church!

Rising like a monument in the desert, the Lancaster Baptist Church has been a beacon of light and a wellspring of hope for thousands of souls over the past quarter of a century.

You are to be commended for the life you have surrendered to God for Him to use in such a marvelous way. Your ministry has not only blessed the lives of thousands of people within the framework of the church's ministry, but it has touched lives across America and areas of the world.

Lancaster Baptist Church is a miracle of God's grace, and heaven's population will be increased as a result of your love for the souls of mankind. I pray that you will have many more years to serve our Lord, not only in Lancaster, but also to the ends of the earth.

May the Lord enrich your life, enhance your ministry, and enlarge your vision.

Until the trumpet sounds, keep a sharp Sword, a bended knee, and an eye on the sky! Keep looking up—He's coming soon! It is in the Book, and God wrote the Book!

Prayerfully,

Raymond W. Barber

Galatians 6:14

Pastor Emeritus: Worth Baptist Church
President Emeritus: Independent Baptist Fellowship International
Chancellor: Crown SW/Norris Seminary

# SALEM BAPTIST TEMPLE
*God will make a way*

February 4, 2011

Dr. Paul Chappell
Lancaster Baptist Church
4020 E. Lancaster Blvd.
Lancaster, CA 93535

Dr. Chappell,

It is with heart-felt seriousness and tremendous appreciation that I write to express a sincere congratulation on the 25th Anniversary of Lancaster Baptist Church. Only eternity will ever be able to reveal the influence of your ministry. By your faithfulness to follow the leadership of our Lord Jesus Christ, He has been able to accomplish marvelous things for His glory.

I thank you for being the pastor of my three daughters, providing a church where they could grow and serve the Lord while attending West Coast Baptist College. Thank you for praying for them, for a genuine staff of people to teach them to prepare for the ministry, and allowing them to earn their way through college through your Pastor's scholarships.

You have been an encouragement, a motivator, a provider of hope, a giver of strength and a source of inspiration for twenty five years. Many have continued on in the Lord's work and found direction through your ministry and walk with God. I pray that you will continue being all God would have you to be, to know His will, and to give Christ the honor for all things.

With many thanks until He comes,

Pastor Stephen A. Brown
Salem, Oregon

Pastor Stephen A. Brown
5412 Liberty Rd. SE Salem, OR 97306
P.O. Box 13766 Salem, OR 97309
www.salembaptisttemple.org
503.581.0994

# CENTRAL BAPTIST CHURCH

Dr. B.G. Buchanan, Sr., Pastor
B.G. Buchanan, Jr., Associate

17017 Florida Blvd. Baton Rouge, LA 70819
P.O. Box 45549 Baton Rouge, LA 70895

January 27, 2011

Dr. Paul Chappell, Pastor
Lancaster Baptist Church
4020 E. Lancaster Blvd.
Lancaster, CA 93535

Dear Dr. Chappell,

It is with great joy that I write a few lines to commemorate your 25th Anniversary. You are a true friend and I am thankful that you are a King James Bible man and also an Independent Baptist that is separated to and for the Word of God. I am thankful for what you are attempting to do through your Church and College for America and the World.

I wanted to thank you again for allowing me to preach in your college chapel a couple of times. It is always a joy.

Thanks also for the many books you have sent my way. I certainly have gotten many blessings from your book "A Daily Word". I have used it many times in my preaching. The "Baptist Voice" has also inspired me in many ways.

Thanks for being such a great mentor for Bro. Daniel and Mrs. Jennifer Hopkins and their family.

May the Lord give you many more productive years at Lancaster Baptist Church and the city to which God has called you.

If I can do anything for you, please, let me know.

Sincerely, as we look for Christ's soon return,

B.G. Buchanan
1 Corinthians 16:18

BGB:sb

*"The Difference is Worth the Drive"*

Phone: (225) 272-5592
Web: www.centralbaptistbr.org

Fax: (225) 272-6400
Email: office@cbc.brcoxmail.com

January 28, 2011

Pastor Paul Chappell
Lancaster Baptist Church
4020 E. Lancaster Blvd.
Lancaster, CA 93535

Dear Pastor Chappell,

I want to congratulate you on twenty-five years of pastoral ministry at Lancaster Baptist Church. Your faithfulness as a pastor and leader has been used to encourage men like myself throughout this country and abroad. Your vision to start West Coast Baptist College has given local churches like ours a place to send young people to be trained for the ministry without fear of compromise. Your example of servant leadership has been a model to both inspire and challenge. Your faithful family has shown that "it can be done" in the home as well. You have been an encouraging friend through the years and I am so happy you have reached this milestone in ministry. My God give you many more years of success as you labor with the fine people of Lancaster Baptist Church.

Your friend,

Tim Butler
Pastor

**FAIRFAX BAPTIST Temple**

Glorify God & Evangelize the World

March 29, 2011

Pastor Paul Chappell
Lancaster Baptist Church
4020 E. Lancaster Blvd.
Lancaster, CA 93535

Dear Pastor Chappell,

Please accept my congratulations on such a wonderful milestone in your life! You are to be commended for twenty-five years as pastor of Lancaster Baptist Church; a testimony of God's goodness and grace. You have my thanks, and the gratitude of many for responding to God's call to Lancaster. Only now, I am sure, after having walked in the Spirit for these many years are you able to see how marvelously God has blessed and I am confident will continue to bless!

Your steadfastness and commitment to the Lord's work shines through as a brilliant jewel in a dark world. Thank you for never looking back or settling for anything less than God's best in your life and the life of LBC. No question about it, God has raised you up as an example of what He can do when a man is fully surrendered to the will of God and His empowering.

I marvel at how the Lord has so gifted and equipped you for His service, and I am privileged to see how you have been such a good steward of God's gifts. Just as remarkable is the wonderful and talented wife with whom God blessed you. All of us in the pastorate realize that it is impossible for us to fulfill God's calling in our lives without the help, support, and dedication of a God-fearing wife. Thank you Terrie!

I count it an honor to have you as a friend and co-laborer in the Lord's great harvest. May God continue to keep His hand upon you as you begin the next twenty-five years of serving the Lord at Lancaster Baptist Church.

In His Name,

*Bud Calvert*

Bud Calvert,
A Servant of God

BC:th
*Personally dictated, but signed in his absence.*

Dr. Troy R. Calvert, Pastor · Dr. Bud R. Calvert, Founder
6401 Missionary Lane, Fairfax Station, VA 22039-1859 · 703.323.8100 · FBTministries.org

**FAIRFAX BAPTIST** *Temple*

*Ministerial Offices*

6401 Missionary Lane
Fairfax Station, VA 22039-1859

tel. 703.323.8100
fax. 703.250.8660

FBTMinistries.org

Troy R. Calvert, Pastor
Dr. Bud Calvert, Founder

February 18, 2011

Dr. Paul Chappell
Lancaster Baptist Church
4020 E. Lancaster Blvd.
Lancaster, CA 93535

Dear Pastor Chappell,

On behalf of Fairfax Baptist Temple, allow me this opportunity to congratulate you on reaching such a wonderful milestone of 25 years in the ministry at Lancaster Baptist Church! When I think of your life and ministry, although I have not sat under you as my pastor, I think of the verse in Hebrews 13:7 where the writer reminds us of those "…who have spoken unto you the word of God: whose faith follow, considering the end of their conversation." Thank you for having a faith that is not only proclaimed but also practiced. You have been a tremendous encouragement to our church as well as many others around the world. Your ministry has been an example to us of how things can and should be done for our Lord. You have set a standard of excellence that has been a wonderful testimony for our great God.

May the Lord continue to keep His hand of blessing upon you. May He continue to fill you with His power. And may you and your special wife, Terrie, know how grateful we are to count you among our friends.

A Fellow Servant in the Lord,

*Troy R. Calvert*

Troy R. Calvert

TC:sa

# Bible Baptist Church

*REACHING PEOPLE... CHANGING LIVES!*

April 4, 2011

Dr. Paul Chappell, Pastor
Lancaster Baptist Church
4020 E. Lancaster Blvd.
Lancaster, CA 93535

Dear Brother Chappell,

Let me commend you and Lancaster Baptist Church on twenty-five years of ministry together. Your leadership and example among independent Baptists in our nation is making a difference. This example is showing others that God deserves excellence in our ministry and service for Him. Lancaster Baptist Church has a truly global impact for the cause of Christ.

Thank you for your friendship. I am praying for both you and your church. May the days ahead result in even more glory to God until our Savior comes. May God bless you.

For Him,

Dr. Mark Campbell, Pastor

Dr. Mark Campbell, Pastor
Rev. Bruce Hancock, Assitant Pastor
Rev. Steve Kinman, Assistant Pastor
Rev. Ryan Livingston, Student Pastor
Rev. Fabio Betancourth, Spanish Pastor

2113 Morgan Johnson Rd   Bradenton, FL 34208   941.746.6221   fax - 941.746.1465   www.4bbc.org

# Faith Baptist Church

Dan Carr, Pastor
8467 Canal Road
Gulfport, MS 39503-9042
**Phone (228) 863-6993**

Dear Bro. Chappell,

**CONGRATULATIONS** on your celebration of 25 years at Lancaster Baptist Church. God's hand of blessing is evident in your life and ministry. My prayer is that God continues to bless and use you and your family in a great and mighty way.

Thank you for your godly example to others, especially during difficult times. Independent Baptist, as a whole, are grateful for all that you do for the cause of Fundamentalism. Above all, thank you for your dedication and faithfulness to our Lord.

Because He Lives,

Pastor Dan Q. Carr, Sr.
Galatians 6:9

1515 Wistar Road
Fairless Hills, PA 19030
(215) 946-7550
www.faithbaptistministries.com
Pastor David W. Cashman

Dear Bro. Chappell,

Congratulations on your 25th Anniversary at Lancaster Baptist Church! My, how the Lord has blessed in those years. What a wonderful example of the movement of God upon a place that has a leader that is willing to serve and sacrifice for his Savior and the people that are placed under his care.

Some want to be leaders of men while others are willing to be their servants. Thank you for allowing the Lord to use you to serve the people of the Antelope Valley and, at the same time, serve thousands of other local churches.

Your influence upon me and the wonderful church I Pastor cannot be properly evaluated. Only in Heaven will we see the true impact of how God has used you to help Faith Baptist Church grow to serve the Lord in a greater way.

Of course, Terrie and your children have had a great part in the work as well. They need to be commended for their willingness to allow you to be what God called you to be. At the same time they have been wonderful examples to my wife and children.

May the Lord give you many more years of faithful and effective service for His glory. May we strive together for the faith. God bless you!

Your friend,

David W. Cashman
Senior Pastor

DC:rt

July 10, 2011

Dr. Paul Chappell
Lancaster Baptist Church
4020 E. Lancaster Blvd.
Lancaster, CA 93535

Dear Paul,

I am thrilled to congratulate you on twenty-five years of ministry at Lancaster Baptist Church! It has been a joy to see both your personal and church ministry influence the lives of so many around you, including me.

As your brother, I find your faithfulness to the Lord has been a constant encouragement to me! As a pastor, I know that much fruit will abound to your account as a result of a life fully invested in serving our Saviour. I have admired your service and dedication for the Lord as I have had the privilege to observe it personally.

The genuine and Christ-like testimony that you and Terrie have displayed have been a great blessing. Thank you for allowing the Lord to use you as He has, and may God richly bless you as you continue to serve Him in the years to come!

In Christ,

Steve Chappell
Pastor

# Solid Rock Baptist Church

CHARLES CLARK JR., PASTOR ✦ CHARLES CLARK III, PASTOR

420 SOUTH WHITE HORSE PIKE
BERLIN, NEW JERSEY 08009

February 17, 2011

Dear Brother Chappell,

Congratulations to you, your family, and the people of Lancaster Baptist for 25 years of God's blessings on the church and ministry there. Thank God that He is still building His Church!

Thank you for the impact that you and your people have had on Solid Rock Baptist Church. Your personal example has inspired us to be much better in the work of the Lord. Your burden to help independent Baptist pastors, their families, and ministries to excel for God's honor and glory is much appreciated. We are indebted for the things we have learned from Striving Together lessons, Leadership Conferences, publications, and the Lancaster Baptist church staff.

West Coast Baptist College is a great place for our young people to train for the ministry. We are especially grateful for the sacrifices made by you and your people in providing the college. God has used West Coast to help train servants of the Lord who are now impacting the Northeast Corridor, where our church is located.

It is an awesome thing to observe God's touch on a pastor and church family. Thank you for obeying the Bible, emphasizing soulwinning, and taking a stand for God in a growing age of apostasy. We appreciate your Biblical position and we stand "striving together" with you and your church family. We are looking forward to watching what God is going to do in the years to come at the Lancaster Baptist Church.

Once again, congratulations, and thank you for being our friend.

In Christ,

Pastor Charles Clark, Jr.
Pastor Charles Clark III

856-767-5056 . solidrockbaptist.org      "...FOR THE WORD OF GOD, AND FOR THE TESTIMONY OF JESUS CHRIST." Revelation 1:9

Dr. Darrell Cox

Pastor

(336) 284 – 2404 – Office

2722 US Hwy. 601 S ♦ Mocksville, NC 27028

*"The fruit of the righteous is a tree of life; and he that winneth souls is wise." Proverbs 11:30*

February 7, 2011

Dr. Paul Chappell
Lancaster Baptsit Church
4020 E. Lancaster Blvd.
Lancaster, CA  93535

Dear Brother Chappell,

Congratulations on reaching another milestone in your ministry of twenty-five years as pastor and founder of the Lancaster Baptist Church.  It is unbelievable to see what God has used you to do in twenty-five years.

I have been there on several occasions to preach in your great college.  I have seen the buildins God has allowed you to build and have heard of the many lives that have been transformed and changed.  It is so amazing to see how God has used you in such a great way.

You are one of my heroes.  Many times while speaking to other pastors, I will tell them of the work you are doing there in Lancaster, California.

Keep up the good work!  We need you because you are so vital to the Independent Baptist in our day.  It's so good to see a man that still stands by the Old Time Religion, when so many have changed and gone to the left.

I love you and will continue to pray for you.  If I can ever be a help to you, please let me know.

Your Friends in Christ,

Darrell Cox, Pastor
TRINITY BAPTIST CHURCH

DRC: mb

SAM DAVISON

March 9, 2011

Pastor Paul Chappell
Lancaster Baptist Church
4020 East Lancaster Blvd.
Lancaster, CA 93535

Dear Bro. Chappell:

After nearly 45 years of ministry, I have reflected upon the big picture to determine what matters most; to determine what is most gratifying. I have come to this conclusion: To be a part of what is so obviously *God's* doing is most fulfilling.

For 25 years you have been a part of what God has chosen to do in and through Lancaster Baptist Church. I rejoice with you and offer my sincere congratulations to you and Lancaster Baptist Church as you reflect upon His workings of this past quarter century.

However, we should only pause now and then, with gratitude, to consider the past. God is still working and so long as He gives strength, let us determine to focus upon continuing to be a part of *His* doings.

I pray the 25th year celebration will bring praise to our Lord and Saviour and at the same time be a blessing to you and Terri, as well as the entire church family.

Your Fellow Servant,

Sam Davison

Pastor Emeritus, Southwest Baptist Church
1300 SW 54th Street · Oklahoma City, OK 73119 · 405-682-1491

President, Heartland Baptist Bible College
4700 NW 10th Street · Oklahoma City, OK 73127 · 405-943-9330
Cell: 405-664-1133 · Email: Sam.Davison@swbaptist.org

# Treasure Valley Baptist Church

### 1300 S. Teare Avenue (Facing I-84) Meridian, ID 83642 • (208) 888-4545

Rick DeMichele, SR. PASTOR

Kendall Doty, ASST. PASTOR • Ruben Garcia, ASST. PASTOR • David Potts, ASST. PASTOR

**Independent**
**Bible Believing**
**Evangelistic**

Sunday School 9:15 am
Morning Worship 10:30 am
  Junior Church
Sunday Evening 6:00 pm
Wednesday Evening 7:00 pm
  Master Club 6:30 pm
Saturday Men's Prayer 8:00 pm

Staffed Nursery

Treasures of Truth
Radio Broadcast
790 AM : 7:45 am
94.1 FM: 10:45 am
94.1 FM: 5:15 pm
(Monday – Friday)

Bearing Precious Seed
Bible Institute
Bookstore
Bus Ministry
Choir Adult/Youth
Christian School
College & Career
Discipleship Class
Fair Booth Ministry
Golden Gems
Group Bible Study
High School Jr/Sr
Hockey Ministries International
Home School Ministry
Jail & Prison Ministry
Jude 22 Ministry
Master Club
Missions
Nursing Home Ministry
Outdoorsmen Ministry
Pastors School
Reformers Unanimous
Rescue Mission Ministry
Sign Ministry
Street Evangelism
Veterans Home Ministry
Young Marrieds
Youth Camps

**LOCATION:**
**Entrance off Overland**
**Between Meridian Rd**
**& Locust Grove**

January 26, 2011

Dear Bro. Chappell & Lancaster Baptist Church.

Congratulation on 25 years as a church family. Being a *long-timer* myself, I appreciate what kind of staying power goes into that kind of longevity. Lancaster Baptist Church and West Coast Baptist College have impacted Christianity worldwide.

Thank you for your faithful example.

A friend in Christ,

Rick DeMichele

RD/lr

I Cor. 15:58

*"He that hath the Son hath Life."* 1 Jn. 5:12
*A BIBLE BELIEVING CHURCH*
**www.tvbc.org**

Dr. Paul Chappell
Lancaster Baptist Church
4020 East Lancaster Blvd.
Lancaster, CA 93535

Dear Dr. Chappell,

Congratulations to you and the Lancaster Baptist Church family on this wonderful 25th Anniversary. It is simply amazing to consider all that God has done for you and through the ministry in these twenty-five fruitful years. To God be the glory!

Beyond congratulations, let me offer a word of appreciation for how you and the Lancaster church family have allowed the blessings of God on the ministry, to be a blessing to other pastors and churches in so many ways. Though we may be separated by a continent, you have made us feel like we are part of a close community. Thank you for your friendship and the "serving others" attitude that so permeates Lancaster Baptist Church.

May God's richest blessing continue to be on you personally, your family, and Lancaster Baptist Church.

In Christ,

Pastor Michael E. Edwards

Pastor Michael Edwards
14510 Spriggs Road
Woodbridge, VA
22193

Phone: (703) 680-6629
Fax: (703) 670-4369
VisitHeritage.com

Home of Heritage
Christian School

"Thy testimonies have I taken as an HERITAGE forever;
for they are the rejoicing of my heart."
Psalm 119:111

**Grace**
BAPTIST CHURCH

March 16, 2011

Dr. Paul Chappell
Lancaster Baptist Church
4020 Lancaster Blvd.
Lancaster, CA 93535

Dear Brother Chappell,

I rejoice with you on your landmark twenty-fifth year anniversary at Lancaster Baptist Church. Twenty-five years of Christian "exceptionalism," Christ-honoring integrity and consecrated service to our Lord and Savior Jesus Christ is a great accomplishment. There are few men that have maintained such balance and strength of stand in the Scriptures and in the ranks of fundamentalism. I have been blessed to observe the extraordinary love you and Terrie have for your staff and for your people in general. You have been exceedingly kind and encouraging to me personally and to a multitude of other pastors across this United States and throughout the globe.

Thank you again for being our honored guest speaker for our 50th Anniversary on July 25, 2010. It was also a delight to have Terrie and your son Matt with us on that special day. Matt is an extraordinary young man that God is going to greatly use. Both Sunday services were the highlight of the year for our church and the Lord blessed and allowed us to see many wonderful decisions made for the cause of Christ, to God be the glory!

My brother, the Lord has raised you up for such a time as this. I have the deepest respect for you and your ministry and I stand by your side in the defense of the gospel. Thank you finally for the ministry of West Coast Baptist College. Our students love the school and have an increased passion for the Word of God, for prayer and for the souls of the lost and dying. Keep on fighting the good fight of the faith; we are on the winning side!!!

Your brother and friend in Christ,

Dr. Bill Egerdahl
Pastor

PACIFIC
BAPTIST CHURCH
"A Family Friendly Church"

February 8, 2011

Dear Pastor Chappell,

Congratulations on 25 years of faithful ministry to the Lord! The work that God has allowed you to do both in the Lancaster area and around the globe has certainly been a God-breathed work! We thank you for the blessing and encouragement you have been to our church personally. Your zeal for the Lord and growing His kingdom challenges us to strive for greater heights for the Lord.

May God bless you, your wife, and family as you continue carrying out the amazing work that God has given you to accomplish for the Kingdom.

Your Friend,

Joe Esposito
JE:jl

3332 Magnolia Ave. | Long Beach, CA 90806 | 562.424.7714 | VisitUs@PacificBaptist.com | www.pacificbaptist.com
Dr. Joe Esposito, Pastor

# LIGHTHOUSE

### Baptist Church

Dear Pastor Chappell,

Congratulations on reaching 25 years of faithful ministry at the Lancaster Baptist Church. What a tremendous testimony for your people, the community, and the students to see God honor your steadfast labors over the years. As your church remembers the various stages of growth, I am sure they will remember the personal sacrifice, prayer, devotion, and time that you have given to make it to this honorable milestone in the ministry.

Let me also congratulate your wife as this is her accomplishment as well. Mrs. Chappell, thank you for being faithful and supporting your husband throughout these many years of ministry. May this celebration bring you the same joy of accomplishment and gratitude to our Lord for the many blessings given to you and the family.

Lastly I want to thank you personally, Br. Chappell, for being a friend to me in ministry. I mean this when I say it, you have been a tremendous encouragement to me and my wife. You have also been a help to our church family and staff through your publications and preaching, and that also means a great deal to me. We are praying for you and the family and I look forward to many more years of service together in Southern California.

Your friend and fellow laborer,

Doug Fisher
Senior Pastor

1345 Skyline Drive, Lemon Grove, Ca 91945 ●(619) 461-5561●Fax (619) 462-1093
http://www.lighthousebaptist.com ● Doug Fisher, Pastor

# CLEVELAND
## BAPTIST CHURCH

PREACHING CHRIST • REACHING THE WORLD

February 8, 2011

Dr. Paul Chappell
Lancaster Baptist Church
4020 E. Lancaster Boulevard
Lancaster, California 93535

Dear Bro. Chappell,

I would like to offer congratulations to you and Terrie for completing twenty-five years as the pastor and first lady of Lancaster Baptist Church. To God be the glory for the great things He has done since your departure from a secure position in an existing work to lead a small, struggling work in Lancaster. Through your leadership, work, and faith God has built a thriving work in southern California.

Denise and I, as well as our entire church family, are extremely grateful for the influence you and Lancaster Baptist Church have had on us. We have been greatly blessed and helped through your preaching, conferences, music, college and Striving Together Publications. On a personal note, I have been challenged by your friendship and influence on my life. I am thankful for the day God allowed our paths to cross.

We pray this anniversary Sunday and week of celebration will be a time of reflection and rejoicing over all that God has accomplished through your lives. We are all tools in God's hands to accomplish His divine purpose, but truthfully, some tools are just a bit more special. Brother Chappell, you are one of God's choice tools, and our world is positively impacted because you yield your life for the Lord's use.

Our prayers and love are with you during this grand occasion.

Your friend,

Kevin Folger
Pastor

KF/cma

4431 Tiedeman Rd. Brooklyn,Ohio 44144 ● (216) 671-2822
www.clevelandbaptist.org ● Kevin Folger, Pastor

March 7, 2011

Dr. Paul Chappell
Lancaster Baptist Church
4020 E. Lancaster Blvd.
Lancaster, CA 93535

Dear Dr. Chappell,

I want to congratulate you on the celebration of your 25th anniversary as the pastor of Lancaster Baptist Church. This, of course, is a very highly commemorative time for you and the church family.

The Lord has done many great things during these 25 years through your influence, leadership and life. There have been scores of people who have been saved, many who are in full time service, many churches started and thriving, and countless lives who can point to the impact the church and the college have had in their lives.

You are to be commended for the steps of faith and obedience you have made over the years that have helped your church family, and churches like mine. Your gracious spirit, soul winner's heart, and firm biblical stand are trademarks of the Holy Spirit's imprint on your life.

Thank you for being a friend to pastors, evangelists, missionaries and laymen alike. Thank you for your burden for churches being planted and established here on the West Coast. Thank you for instilling great faith and courage in countless servants of God!

Most of all, thank you for your friendship and investment in my life as well. My wife and I are deeply indebted to the friendship that you and Terrie have extended to us over the years.

It is my prayer that the Lord will continue to use you in an even greater way to advance the cause of Christ around the world.

Have a blessed day!

Your Friend,

Alan Fong
Pastor

2960 Merced Street • San Leandro, CA 94577
510.357.7023 • www.hbc.org • Alan Fong, Pastor

February 1, 2011

Bro. Paul Chappell
Lancaster Baptist Church
4020 E. Lancaster Blvd.
Lancaster, CA 93535

Dear Bro. Chappell,

Congratulations are certainly in order for the way that you have used these last 25 years that God has given you. Very few people have likely packed so much into that same period of time. Your use of that time has elevated many more of us by demonstrating what God can do with a man who has a huge vision coupled with clear discipline. It has been a joy to watch it all. Thank you for sharing the lessons that you have learned and the success you have enjoyed with so many others. The benefits have been felt by hundreds of other churches and pastors. I hope that through the busyness and rush of Leadership Conference that you are able to stop long enough to enjoy a little reflection on what God has done. Thank you for the help that you have been to me, personally. I value the investment.

For His glory,

Wayne Hardy

E. Virginia & N. Jardot | P.O. Box 1985 | Stillwater, OK 74076 | stillwaterbbc.org
Phone 405.372.7444 | Fax 405.377.7948 | info@stillwaterbbc.org

January 12, 2011

Dear Pastor Chappell,

Congratulations on 25 years at the Lancaster Baptist Church. I want to thank you personally for following the Lord's will and the impact that one decision has had on so many people; including me and my family.

What an amazing thought; that when you were being led by God to start a local church Bible college He knew that I would be going to attend in January of 1998. Thank you for making the will of God your priority and teaching us to do the same.

The quality of the theological education that my wife and I received was amazing but it pales in comparison to the lessons that we learned from the lives that were lived out before us each and every week. You and your staff taught us what it meant to be a servant leader as well as a soul winner. We learned the definition of fellowship with a purpose and what hospitality looks like from the inside of homes not the inside of classrooms.

Your example and influence on our lives as students goes far beyond the pulpit and has touched our hearts indelibly. Only eternity will reveal all that has come to pass because of one decision: the will of God as the pastor of Lancaster Baptist Church. Thank you for staying faithful to the cause. I love you and am praying for you.

Your Friend,

Kyle Haynes
Pastor
Shadow Mountain Baptist Church

KH/it

LET GOD ARISE
17810 MONTEREY RD. | MORGAN HILL, CA 95037 | 408.782.7806

**Eric Crawford, Pastor**

Dr. Paul Chappell
Lancaster Baptist Church
4020 E. Lancaster Blvd.
Lancaster, CA 93535

Dear Dr. Chappell:

Twenty Five Years!  Nine Thousand One Hundred days and nights!
Congratulations.  Having been a long way down that path, I know the days
have been paradoxical.  One day atop Mount Pisgah overlooking the Promised
Land.  Another day searching the valley of Elah for five smooth stones before
you meet the giant.  Having rejected the armor of man your faith growing
stronger with the selection of each stone.  Then victory came.

In all these days you have been a voice in the wilderness trumpeting out
a warning to flee from the wrath to come.  In Heaven you will no doubt
converse with many who fled to Christ when they heard your voice and saw
your faithfulness.

With this mark of a long journey it is not yet time to stack the weapons
of war.  Press on, Preach on, Fight on, there is more ground to be taken.

I pray that God will give you good health, renewed strength, and a drop of
fresh oil.

Your Friend,

A. V. Henderson

1200 S. Highway 156 • Haslet, Texas 76052 • (817) 439-5220 • www.hbchaslet.org
"that ye may know ... the riches of the glory of his inheritance in the saints" Ephesians 1:15-23

36

# Summerville Baptist Church
## "In His Steps"

February 15, 2011

Dear Dr. Chappell & Lancaster Baptist Church,

I wish to praise God for the twenty-five years of ministry that the Lord has given you together. It is amazing all that the Lord has accomplished with you in these twenty-five years. God is doing some very wonderful and special things on the west coast and around the world through you and your faithfulness; you are being used to His glory. I personally am thankful for how Summerville Baptist Church and I have benefited from your ministry and your influence.

It has been our blessing to enjoy your pulpit ministry here in our own church. We have been blessed by your preaching, by the preaching of several of your staff, as well as by your singing groups. I also have been blessed by attending the Spiritual Leadership Conference and other special events there on your campus. It has been a blessing to have several of our students attend the college there including my daughter and son-in-law. I am blessed that two of my children are members in the church there and under your ministry. It has been a blessing to benefit from many of the books published by Striving Together Publications, as well as the Adult Educational Materials.

I appreciate the commitment that you have to the Lord, to His Word, and to making a difference in the world. Your commitment to excellence in the things the Lord leads you do with Him are encouraging. I appreciate your influence, your friendship, and your prayers on my behalf. I want you to know that you and those who serve with you are in my prayers as well. Let us keep striving together for the glory of the Lord in our lives and through our lives.

Your Friend in the Faith.

Franklin E. Humber, Pastor

1 PETER 2:21
"FOR EVEN HEREUNTO WERE YE CALLED:
BECAUSE CHRIST ALSO SUFFERED FOR US,
LEAVING US AN EXAMPLE,
THAT YE SHOULD FOLLOW HIS STEPS:"

PO Box 164 * First & Jefferson * Summerville, OR 97876 * (541) 534-9155

# Sauk Trail
BAPTIST TEMPLE

4411 Sauk Trail | PO Box 347
Richton Park, IL 60471
708.481.1490, www.stbt.org

January 17, 2011

Dr. Paul Chappell
Lancaster Baptist Church
4020 East Lancaster Boulevard
Lancaster, CA 93535

Dear Brother Chappell,

Congratulations to you and your church as you celebrate your 25th Anniversary!!!

I am not in your inner circle and hardly on the fringe of your camp and yet I have been the recipient of God's blessings overflowing from the California desert!

I sent my staff to a leadership conference, and they came back different. What I tried to teach in a decade, they saw in a week, and became an asset and help to me in our church. I have had several students benefit from your college as well. Then in December of 2009 I had the privilege of preaching in chapel to the student body, and what a joy it was. Though I was sick and physically limited, the students were attentive and responsive to the preaching of the Word. WOW ... another blessing. We have also used your printed material ... thanks for your faithfulness in every area of ministry God has given you.

When I first heard of Lancaster Baptist Church and it's growth and size I wondered if it was another Baptist Cult or a Big-Time Compromise ... and was I thrilled to find out it was truly a Fundamental Baptist Church! It's nice to see a big trophy of God's grace standing as tall as the mountains surrounding Lancaster! It is also refreshing to find a church that is old fashioned in standards, music, soul winning, preaching and BAPTIST doctrine and at the same time NOT MAD ABOUT IT! Your people are so kind, helpful, and Christlike ... it is truly an oasis in the desert for a thirsty soul.

May God give you another 25, that the world may know ...

Sincerely,

Bruce M. Humbert
John 17:23

THAT THE WORLD
MAY KNOW
JOHN 17:23

**AMBASSADOR**
BAPTIST CHURCH
*enriching lives through Christ*

March 6, 2011

Pastor Paul Chappell
Lancaster Baptist Church
4020 E. Lancaster Blvd
Lancaster CA 93535

Dear Pastor Chappell,

Congratulations! Twenty-five years of serving the Lord in full-time ministry is a great testimony to the grace of God at work in your life. The Lord has used you to impact so many lives across this state and around the world. I thank God often for your influence upon my life as well.

Your willingness to follow the leading of the Lord to plant the Lancaster Baptist Church, and found West Coast Baptist College has been an encouragement to all of us. May the Lord continue to use you and your dear wife, Terrie, in a special way there in Southern California.

Every time I have the privilege to be around you, your spirit encourages my heart. Your faithfulness to the ministry is to be commended. May God grant you many more fruitful years of service to Him. If there is ever anything I can do for you, please do not hesitate to let me know.

Your Friend,

Pastor Irmler
Ambassador Baptist Church

JMI:bi

3354 W. Clinton Ave | Fresno, CA 93722 | 559.275.0681 | ambassador4you.com | Joshua M. Irmler, Pastor

# PASTORS J–R

# Community Baptist Church

## Home of Community Baptist Christian School

March 1, 2011

Pastor Paul Chappell
4020 E. Lancaster Blvd.
Lancaster, CA 93535

Dear Brother Chappell:

Congratulations on 25 years as Pastor of Lancaster Baptist Church.

Your vision has inspired many of us for His cause and will have a perpetual effect on the future of Fundamentalism. You are a blessing, brother, as is the wonderful work God has raised up there in Lancaster.

Keep on keeping on and may God strengthen and encourage your heart.

In Christ,

Dr. Doug Jackson

Dr. Douglas R. Jackson
Community Baptist Church

drj:mrl

8331 Gratiot Road, Saginaw, MI 48609 · Phone: (989) 781-2340 · Fax: (989) 781-1344

Dr. Douglas R. Jackson, Pastor

# First Baptist
# Church
of Rosemount

**14400 Diamond Path West
ROSEMOUNT, MINNESOTA 55068
Phone 651-423-2271 ~ Fax 651-423-4471
www.fbcrosemount.org**

February 7, 2011

**MINISTRIES:**

Christian School

Bus

Sunday School

Youth

Music

Children's Church

Nursing Home

Missionary

Soulwinning

Summer Camp

Jail

Master Club

Deaf

Spanish

Reformers Unanimous

Dr. Paul Chappell
Lancaster Baptist Church
4020 Lancaster Blvd.
Lancaster, CA 93535

Dear Brother Chappell:

It does not seem possible that Lancaster Baptist Church is celebrating it's 25th anniversary this year. As I look back over those twenty-five years I am hard pressed to name another fundamental, independent Baptist church that has accomplished what you and your people have accomplished.

As you move forward into a new quarter of a century of ministry my prayer is that God will continue to bless you like He has over the past 25 years. No doubt your love for lost souls and the preaching of the Word of God has been supreme. Your keen awareness of administrative skills is a gift that the Lord has blessed you with. Therefore, let me encourage you to continue the close walk you have maintained with Him in prayer as you continue to press on as the Savior tarries His coming and gives you life. Needless to say you and your ministry has been a great blessing to me and it has been a joy to watch what your ministry has done in the life of so many of our young people who have attended West Coast Baptist College.

Congratulations on 25 years of glorious ministry and may God grant you many more as you continue to faithfully serve Him. With best wishes and personal kindest regards I remain:

Sincerely your friend & co-laborer,

Dr. Ed Johnson
Pastor Emeritus

EJ/pjd

*"Come Grow With Us"*

# VICT🌐RY
### BAPTIST CHURCH

January 16<sup>th</sup>, 2011

Bro. Chappell,

Congratulations on twenty-five years of ministry in one place! This *is* something to be celebrated. It is a great example and a testimony of the faithfulness of our Lord. I am sure you have many wonderful memories, exciting stories, and thrilling victories after all of these years!

I am sure you will hear many testimonies from the many lives you have influenced in this span of time. It is an honor to share with you how you have touched my life and ministry. We have only met on a few occasions and do not know each other well, but I can say that you have been a strong influence. In fact, I have told my wife on several occasions that your ministry has probably impacted me more than the Bible College I attended!

One of the ways you have been influential that stands, in my mind, is your desire to befriend preachers. I am very thankful for this. When so many have decided to be divisive, you have decided to be friendly, without compromising. This stand has allowed me to be your friend. It is encouraging to a young preacher (33 years old) to know that there is someone I can look to for help and encouragement.

Another significant trait is your balance. Your philosophy of ministry, which is really just a biblical philosophy, is one of balance. Soul-winning *and* discipleship; service *and* leadership; grace *and* truth are all areas in which you have been an example. Thank you for placing an emphasis on these oft neglected areas!

MICHAEL JONES, *Pastor*

We recently sent the first (hopefully not the last!) young person from our church to WCBC. This is a long way from Roanoke Rapids, NC! But we have been very pleased with the care and training that he has received while he has been away. Thank you for the investment you are making in the lives of so many young people!

Although most of your influence has been indirect, I would like to thank you for helping me be a better-equipped servant of the Lord. It is a privilege to count you as my friend. I pray that God will give you many more years of service in Lancaster. It truly is a miracle in the desert!

Keep on keeping on. If there is ever anything I can do for you please let me know.

Your friend,

Pastor Michael Jones
Victory Baptist Church
Roanoke Rapids, NC

the
CHURCH
that **ACTS**

January 13, 2011

Pastor Paul Chappell
Lancaster Baptist Church
4020 E. Lancaster Blvd.
Lancaster, CA 93535

Dear Pastor Chappell,

Congratulations on your 25th anniversary there at Lancaster Baptist Church!

I'm sure it is obvious to everyone in Lancaster the impact you have had on that city and even on the state of California. You have also impacted the rest of our country and even the world. I know you have had a great influence in my life, my ministry and my family. I will be sending my third child to West Coast Baptist College in the fall. I know that my family and my ministry are better because of you. I can even say the city of Glen Burnie, Maryland is better because of what God has used you to do. Thank you so much for the influence on my life.

May the Lord richly bless you.

Sincerely in Christ,

Pastor King

GRANITE BAPTIST CHURCH | Senior Pastor Curtis King
7823 Oakwood Road | Glen Burnie, MD 21061 | 410.761.1352 | www.granitebaptist.org

PAUL KINGSBURY, PASTOR

**May 12, 2011**

**Dr. Paul Chappell**
**West Coast Baptist College**
4010 E. Lancaster Blvd.
Lancaster, California 93535

**Dear Brother & Mrs. Paul Chappell,**

Congratulations Pastor and Mrs. Chappell, and the members of Lancaster Baptist Church for 25 years of Christ honoring excellence in ministry to the Antelope Valley of California and to the world. We commend Pastor Chappell for a job well done and anticipate the wonderful prospects of another quarter of a century of reaching people with the good news of the gospel, discipling believers and training Christian workers for the global harvest field.

*Your friend and co-laborer,*

**Paul Kingsbury**
PAK/ll

5301 E. Riverside Boulevard • Rockford, IL 61114 • 815-877-6021 • FAX 815-877-6076 • www.northlove.org

*"Beloved, if God so loved us, we ought also to love one another." 1 John 4:11*

# Junction City Baptist Church

Adam Langston
Church Planter

But none of these things move me, neither count I my life dear unto myself, so that I might finish my course with joy, and the ministry, which I have received of the Lord Jesus, to testify the gospel of the grace of God.

Acts 20:24

February 7, 2011

Pastor Paul Chappell
Lancaster Baptist Church
4020 E. Lancaster Blvd
Lancaster, CA 93535

Dear Pastor Chappell,

As a former member and staff of Lancaster Baptist Church, and graduate of West Coast Baptist College, it is with great joy and delight to say thank you and congratulations for your faithfulness to the Lord and the ministry for 25 years at the Lancaster Baptist Church.

I am so grateful to the Lord for what you have allowed Him to do through your life. **The Lord has used your life and ministry to impact my life in a huge way.** Your life and leadership has been a genuine model and a Godly example for any Christian to follow.

As a young Titus or Timothy in the ministry, may I commend you for your continuous sacrifice and committed service to our Lord and Savior Jesus Christ! Your faithfulness to the Lord and the ministry continues to inspire many young preachers to keep pressing on for the cause of Christ.

**May the Lord give you many more fruitful years of serving Him!**

I love you Pastor!

Sincerely in Christ,

*Adam Langston*

Adam Langston
Pastor

**Sending Church:**
Harvest Baptist Church
2615 Farm Bureau Rd.
Manhattan, KS 66502
jointheharvest.org
785.539.8174

junctioncitybaptist.org | 785.223.2565 | adam.langston@yahoo.com

*High Street*
Baptist Church

7399 N. High Street
Columbus, OH 43235

Charles E. Mainous III
*Pastor*

February 15, 2011

Pastor Chappell
Lancaster Baptist Church
4020 E. Lancaster Blvd.
Lancaster, CA  93535

Dear Pastor Chappell,

*I Timothy 5:17 "Let the elders that rule WELL be counted worth of double honour."*

Words cannot express how blessed, inspired, and spiritually challenged I am by your amazing life and ministry.

Your sacrifice of love and servant's heart are only rivaled by your diligent determination. I admire you greatly for all you have been able to accomplish for the glory of God in twenty-five short years.

God has definitely put His anointing and power upon your life.  I just wanted to let you know how thankful I am for your personal testimony of character, integrity, and selflessness.  I count it a privilege  to serve with you in this generation.

My prayer is that God will multiply His work there in Lancaster, California, and that a multitude of souls will be impacted for eternity.

Happy Anniversary.

In His love,

Pastor Mainous, III

CEM/lb

HIGHSTREET
BAPTISTCHURCH

*www.highstreetbaptistchurch.com*

**106 E Shields Ave • Fresno, CA 93704**

January 21, 2011

Pastor Paul Chappell
Lancaster Baptist Church
4020 E. Lancaster Blvd.
Lancaster, CA    93535

Brother Chappell:

Congratulations on 25 years of ministry there in Lancaster! I can still remember the early reports of God's blessing there, nearly a quarter of a century ago. It seems like just yesterday that we were informed that Dr. Goetsch would be coming on staff to help in the college ministry. I had a young person in my church who was determined to go to Maranatha Baptist Bible College, where her pastor and pastor's wife had graduated. But I could sense that there was something unique about the ministry there and was thrilled that we would no longer have to send our young adults across the country to go to Bible college. That young lady's future would forever be impacted because of her decision to attend college there. By the way, she married your (then) new vice-president. Her name was April Averbeck (Goetsch)......

Your ministry has been a blessing to my own in so many ways. The college has been such a help to churches like ours, long hoping to have something here on the Western portion of the country. As you know, most all of our graduates attend WCBC and its benefit to my own children cannot be expressed in words. I want to thank you for your personal investment in my kids, and for your pastoral leadership as they have moved away from home. Your annual Leadership Conference and school-sponsored Fine Arts Competitions have challenged and encouraged us all!

Thank you for your friendship and support of ministries like ours all over the country. May the Lord not only give you many more rewarding years of service there, but also use you and your staff to raise up the next generation of Christian servants. God bless you, Brother Chappell. Though I have not often said so in the past, I truly appreciate all that you do!

Your Friend,

*Chuck Miller*

Pastor Chuck Miller

**Chuck Miller** • *Senior Pastor*          Church Office: **559.226.2222**
**Joel Rockey** • *Outreach Pastor*        Fax: **559.226.7785**
**Jake Hargrave** • *Youth Pastor*         Academy Office: **559.226.7784**          www.faithbaptistfresno.org

# Franklin Road
# BAPTIST CHURCH
## *M i n i s t r i e s*

*Dr. Mike Norris, Pastor*

January 31, 2011

Dear Dr. Chappell,

I wanted to write you on this special day and say congratulations on 25 years of ministry at the Lancaster Baptist Church! What a milestone! Many have come to Christ in the Antelope Valley because of the sacrifice of you and your wife many years ago. I have heard your testimony many times as you have preached. Those early years of labor have now paid off, and you and your people enjoy a worldwide ministry. To God be the glory!

Through your example and effort, the Lancaster Baptist Church has become a pattern for soulwinning and discipleship. The Lord has allowed you to have national and international influence. Each time I have the privilege to visit the ministry there, I am captivated by the excitement in the air and challenged to do more for the Lord.

To lead the Church to start the West Coast Baptist College was a tremendous act of faith and wisdom. There is no better place on earth to train preachers than in the hotbed environment of a soulwinning New Testament Church. I am grateful to the people of Lancaster Baptist Church for following their Pastor in this dream. My son, and many of our young people have been students there, and thus, exposed to some of the best instruction and influence of our day.

This is an historical moment in Fundamentalism! To build a Church that reaches thousands in just twenty-five years is a tremendous accomplishment. But to build an Independent, Fundamental, Soulwinning, Separated, Baptist Church in southern California is monumental, if not miraculous!

Bro. Chappell, thank you for your friendship down through the years. On behalf of the people of the Franklin Road Baptist Church in Murfreesboro, Tennessee, congratulations on 25 years of ministry at the Lancaster Baptist Church! May the Lord give you many more years of service.

In Christ,

Pastor Mike Norris

3148 FRANKLIN ROAD ✦ MURFREESBORO, TN 37128 ✦ 615.890.0820 ✦ 615.890.0821 fax ✦ www.frbc.com

# Bible Baptist Church

2432 E. 18th Street, National City, CA 91950
Tel: (619) 267-3761    Fax: (619) 434-2169
Larry Obero, Pastor

February 1, 2011

Dr. and Mrs. Paul Chappell
Lancaster Baptist Church
4020 E. Lancaster Blvd.
Lancaster, CA 93535

Dear Dr. &Mrs. Chappell,

My wife Myrna and I, and the members of Bible Baptist church congratulate you on your 25th year in the ministry preaching the gospel of our Lord and saviour Jesus Christ at Lancaster Baptist Church.

You and Mrs. Chappell have been godly examples for others to follow.

We love you both, and extremely happy for you, your people, Lancaster Baptist Church and West Coast Baptist College, on this special occasion.

Your burden for souls and passion for world missions are noteworthy and inspiring.

Thank you for your friendship and for touching our lives and the lives of many of our co-laborers for God.

We value and treasure your friendship enormously.

Rest assured of our continuous prayers on your behalf.

Sincerely,

Pastor & Mrs. Larry Obero and Bible Baptist Church family

*"Go ye into all the world, and preach the gospel to every creature." Mark 16:15*

# FIRST BAPTIST CHURCH

### THE CHURCH THAT CARES ABOUT YOU

*-PASTOR R.B. OUELLETTE*

March 3, 2011

Dr. Paul Chappell
Lancaster Baptist Church
4020 E Lancaster Blvd.
Lancaster CA 93535

My Dear Brother,

Congratulations on the most amazing twenty-five years of ministry I have ever witnessed. By God's grace, the united cooperation of your people, and your unstinting, unbelievable labor, you have seen more souls saved, more converts discipled, more laborers sent, more workers trained, more ministries started, and more buildings built than most men see in ten lifetimes.

Thank you for preaching, loving, and living the Word of God.

Thank you for sharing your heart, your ministry, and your life with men of God across America and around the world.

Thank you for modeling a spirit-filled, spirit-led walk with God.

Thank you for assuming the burden of training our young people through founding and building West Coast Baptist College.

Thank you for taking a strong stand for the scriptures, soulwinning, and separation.

Thank you for being my friend and allowing me the wonderful privilege of serving with you so many times in so many different places.

I pray that your vision will remain clear, your voice strong, and your vigor undiminished until Jesus comes. I love you very much and am glad for the honor and attention you'll be given at this special celebration. It is but a fraction of what you deserve and but a foretaste of what awaits you on the other side. God bless you.

Your Friend,

R.B. Ouellette, Pastor

---

*2400 King Rd., Saginaw, MI 48601* | *Tel.: 989-777-0210* | *Email: fbcbridgeport@sbcglobal.net*
*P.O. Box 249, Bridgeport, MI 48722* | *Fax: 989-777-7376* | *Web: www.2fbc.com*

"But thanks be to God, which giveth us the victory through our Lord Jesus Christ."
1 Corinthians 15:57

February 14, 2011

Dear Pastor Chappell,

Congratulations on twenty-five years of ministry in Lancaster! The Lord has richly blessed you in so many ways. We praise the Lord for all that has been accomplished through the Lancaster Baptist Church and your ministry. Many lives have been changed as a result of God working through you.

I appreciate so much your fervor, faithfulness, and friendship. Thank you for your fervency for the truths of the Word of God and the labor of the Lancaster Baptist Church to preach these truths to the community. Thank you for your faithfulness to your family, calling, and your Saviour. As a younger preacher I am so thankful for an example I can look up to. Thank you for your friendship. You have always been an encouragement to me. The counsel, suggestions, emails, and just friendly conversations have reminded me that I can respectfully call you a friend.

May God richly bless you as you continue to preach the Gospel of Jesus Christ to a lost and dying world. We love you and Mrs. Chappell and are very thankful for you!

Your Friend,

Rick Owens, Pastor
1 Corinthians 15:57

Pastor Rick Owens • PO Box 8307 • Fresno, CA 93747 • info@fresnovictory.com • (559) 930-2373
www.fresnovictory.com

# Heritage Baptist Church

79 Ardagh Road
Barrie, Ontario  L4N 9B6

| **Church:** | | **Residence:** |
| --- | --- | --- |
| **(705) 733-0097** | **Dr. LeRoy A. Pennell, Pastor** | **(705) 722-0527** |

January 21, 2011

Dear Dr. Paul Chappell:

It is a great joy to be able to greet you and send along some words of encouragement on this special day, when you celebrate the 25th Anniversary of Lancaster Baptist Church.

It is amazing what God has accomplished through you during these special years. I'm sure in the years to come; some will look back at these years of beginning as the 'Good Old Days, when they saw God move in such a miraculous way in the planting of this church.

Lancaster Baptist Church, with their numerous ministries, has been a tremendous blessing and help to so many other churches and pastors. Your ministry has reached far beyond the borders of your city to include the whole world.

May God continue to give you great strength and wisdom for many more years of service and blessing.

Sincerely, or souls,

LeRoy A. Pennell
Pastor
Heritage Baptist Church
Barrie, Ontario, Canada

**FOR WITH GOD NOTHING SHALL BE IMPOSSIBLE  Luke 1:37**

January 17, 2011

DR. GARY RANDALL
SENIOR PASTOR

ELMWOOD
BAPTIST
CHURCH

Dear Pastor Chappell,

Congratulations to you and Terrie on your 25th Ministry Anniversary at Lancaster Baptist Church!

What God has done through your dedication and hard work is such a powerful testimony and encouragement for us all.

Betty and I are so happy for you, and want to say "Thank You" for how you have allowed God to use you to strengthen and bless not only us... but literally thousands across this Nation!

May God continue to bless you greatly, and give you many more fruit-filled years.

Your Friend and brother in Christ,

13100 East 144th Avenue      Brighton, Colorado 80601      tel: 303.659.3818      www.elmwoodbaptist.org

# Hopewell Baptist Church

3755 Linda Vista Avenue
Napa, California 94558
(707) 252-0332

Mike Ray
Pastor

Dear Bro. Chappell,

Congratulations on 25 years of faithful persevering, uncompromising labor for the Lord in Lancaster! You have been a man of God, friend, co-laborer, preacher, soulwinner, husband, father, author, leader of leaders, conference speaker, counselor and Christian. Thank you for showing us all "How to do it".

The only regret I have for your ministry is we never got to fish Cabo together. May that be on top of your goal sheet for the next 25 years! You have been a "Big Shot" who never acted like it. We're proud of you.

Your friend in Napa,

Pastor Mike Ray
MR/cm

Bringing the water of life to the Napa Valley

DR. DAN REED, PASTOR

# HARVEST BAPTIST CHURCH

*"Look on the fields
for they are white
already to harvest."*
*John 4:35*

January 19, 2011

Dr. Paul Chappell,

On this 25th Anniversary of Lancaster Baptist Church, I want to congratulate you and the church there in Lancaster for an amazing ministry that has inspired so many other churches and thousands of fundamental Christians. It has been my privilege to be there and speak and thrill at this modern New Testament church. Truly, what Paul said to the Thessalonians, we can say of you, "You have been an ensample to all…" Thanks for your love of Christ and faithfulness to His Word! Thanks for being a friend!

Your Friend,

Dr. Dan Reed
Harvest Baptist Church
Acworth, Georgia

3460 Kellogg Creek Rd. ◆ Acworth, GA 30102 ◆ (770) 974-9091 ◆ Fax (770) 974-9453

Dear Pastor and Mrs. Chappell,

Wendy and I are honored to be among those you count as friends, and we are thrilled to be able to offer a word of congratulations for the completion of a quarter-century pasorting the Lancaster Baptist Church!

Your example and encouragement have been an immeasurable aid to so many of us serving alongside you in the work of the ministry.

In the sea of ministry there are a good many ships in the fundamental Baptist fleet. They come in different sizes. Some carry large crews and some smaller, but all are moving forward together carrying out our Great Commander's commission. We who skipper the "cruisers" and the "destroyers" and the "tankers" and the "transports" always enjoy the opportunities we have to be piped aboard the "aircraft carriers" like the Lancaster Baptist Church for further training and inspiration.

Though we all expect our Saviour's return before another 25 years passes, we pray your next 25 will bring "much fruit that remaineth."

God bless you, dear Brother Paul, and Sister Terrie. We love and appreciate you!

Sincerely In Jesus,

Bill and Wendy Rench

## Gospel Light Baptist Church

P.O. Box 38   Walkertown   North Carolina  27051

Phone  (336) 722-9700   Fax  (336) 722-5189   Email  staff@glbcs.org   Website  www.glbcs.org

Bobby Roberson, Pastor        Frank Shumate, Assistant Pastor        Tim Hicks, Youth Pastor        Jeff Johnson, Spanish Pastor

January 17, 2011

Dr. Paul Chappell, Pastor
Lancaster Baptist Church
4020 E. Lancaster Blvd.
Lancaster, California 93535

Dear Bro. Paul,

Congratulations to you on 25 years as Pastor of Lancaster Baptist Church. I can say like the Apostle Paul said to the Church of Philippi, "I thank my God upon every remembrance of you."

Through the years I have watched you and feel your motive is like Dr. Lee Roberson who said, "I pray that God will do such a work here that man will have to say it was God and not man who did it."

I am grateful for your friendship through the years and am thankful for your faithfulness. Thank you for not compromising and for taking a stand against the world. My prayer is that the Lord will give you many more years there at Lancaster to preach His Word.

We also appreciate your dear wife, Terri, and the children. As you know, the Pastor's job is much easier when the family's heart is in God's work. May God continue to bless you, your dear family, and the people there at Lancaster Baptist Church.

Your Brother In Christ,

Bobby Roberson

BR:mp

*"To God be the glory, great things He hath done..."*

59

*Let your*
## LIGHT SO SHINE

**Pleasant Valley Baptist Church** | 13539 Garner Lane | Chico, California 95973 | 530.343.0555 | pvbaptist.org | Tim Ruhl, Pastor

March 8, 2011

Bro. Chappell,

Thank you for 25 years of pastoring. Thank you for our friendship which is bigger than life to me. Thank you for going soul winning together. Thank you for praying together. Thank you for crying together. Thank you for allowing me to tag along around the world together. Thank you for introducing me to the hall-of-fame of preachers. Thank you for the many opportunities to preach at Lancaster Baptist Church, West Coast Baptist College, Lancaster Baptist Schools, and the renowned Men and Boys Camp Out. Thank you for influencing my entire family. Thank you for mentoring my sons and daughters. Thank you for loving people. Thank you for loving me. Thank you for looking past my faults. Thank you for your example on which I reflect many times. Thank you for your preaching. Thank you for your teaching. Thank you for your love for the lost. Thank you for laughing with me. Thank you for being trustworthy — that's big in my book and hard to find anymore. Thank you for having character. Thank you for having integrity. Thank you for being real. Thank you for being a friend's friend. Thank you for being a pastor to pastors.

Thank you for never getting too big for certain people. Thank you for your marriage example. Thank you for your family example. Thank you for being Spirit-filled. Thank you for remaining yielded. Thank you for loving the Saviour. Thank you for touching the world . . . you have make it a better place to live. Thank you for knowing that I love you.

Your friend,

Pastor Tim Ruhl

*Let your light so shine before men, that they may see your good works, and glorify your Father which is in heaven.*
*– MATTHEW 5:16*

# PASTORS S–Z

900 Benicia Road
Vallejo, CA 94591
Richard Scudder, Pastor
707-643-0093
www.BibleBaptistVallejo.com

July 2011

Dr. Paul Chappell
Lancaster Baptist Church
4020 E. Lancaster Blvd.
Lancaster, CA 93535

Dear Brother Chappell,

My wife, Barbara, and I congratulate you on your twenty-five years of ministry at Lancaster Baptist Church. Your personal walk with the Lord as a husband, father, pastor and fellow servant of the Lord has touched our lives in so many ways.

You have taught us by word and example the Christ-like life. You have modeled the Spirit-filled life and challenged us to remember the mission, great commission, of the local church is to point lost souls to Christ.

Thank you for your vision and faith to see Independent Fundamental Baptist equipped for ministry. We so appreciate the Ministry of Lancaster Baptist Church, West Coast Baptist College, Striving Together ministry. The publishing of useful books and materials are tools that improve the ministry of other local churches and Christians. We are grateful for your continually giving encouragement by words written and spoken.

Sincerely,

Richard Scudder
Pastor

**Harvest Baptist**
Church

Planting. Watering. Reaping.

January 13, 2011

Pastor Paul Chappell
Lancaster Baptist Church
4020 East Lancaster Boulevard
Lancaster, CA 93535

Dear Bro. Chappell,

In every generation God raises up men who seem to possess both a special discernment for how things are and a sharp vision for how things should be. You are one of those rare men in our generation. God bless you and Terri for selflessly sharing yourselves and your family with our generation. Serving under the proverbial microscope is not without its pressures, but thank you for subjecting yourself to them in order to better serve your people and your contemporaries in the ministry.

Milestones like these allow us a brief opportunity to rest upon them and gaze backward at the grace of God. And, oh, how His grace has enveloped your ministry at Lancaster! Without a doubt, it is a "God thing." But milestones inevitably turn our faces toward the setting sun as we realize anew the shortness of the day and the length of our remaining journey. May these moments of rest, as you bask in the sunlight of grace bestowed, provide a warm sense of God's approval and a bright ray to shine down the path of future blessing.

Thank you for friendship, mentorship, and leadership. May God keep your heart right and your corresponding vision clear. We love you!

Sincerely,

Kurt W. Skelly
Senior Pastor

# Rose Park Baptist Church

**Senior Pastor**
David T. Smith

**Assistant Pastor**
Jim Gerber

**Assistant Pastor**
Jason Smith

**Ministries**

Bus Ministry

Soul Winning
Ministry

Mercy Ministry

Visual\Audio Minis-
try

Children's Ministry

Teen Ministry

Adult &
Discipleship
Ministries

Music Ministry

Discipleship

January 11, 2011

Dear Dr. Chappell,

Congratulations to you and your church for twenty-five years of sharing God's blessings together. You and your church have truly been inspiration and encouragement to thousands of God's people.

Thank you for being an example of caring and powerful leadership. You and your church have helped me in many ways as I seek to serve the Lord here in Michigan. Your leadership lessons have taught me much. Your sermons have blessed me and the Leadership Conference has inspired me. One of the highlights of my life was the opportunity to speak in chapel at West Coast Baptist College. God has blessed you with the heart of a pastor, and you have graciously reached out to other pastors with an influence that says you care and desire to help and encourage others.

Thank you for being a blessing and a friend in the ministry—even though we hardly ever meet up personally. You don't know this, but God introduced me to you and your ministry at a time when I was ready to give up because of all the "infighting" among fundamental Baptists. It was your spirit and ministry that encouraged me to keep on the firing line and to realize we don't have to fight amongst ourselves to get the job done.

You, your family, and your church are to be commended on twenty-five years of effectively doing the work of the ministry. Thank you for your example and encouragement!

In Christ,

Dr. Dave Smith
Pastor

600 Butternut Drive • Holland, Michigan 49424 • (616) 399-2558

# Northstar Baptist Church

Dr. David Sorenson, Pastor

1315 South Arlington Avenue
Duluth, MN 55811
218-726-0209

January 17, 2011

Dr. Paul Chappell
Lancaster Baptist Church
4020 E. Lancaster Blvd.
Lancaster, CA 93535

Dear brother Chappell:

Congratulations on your twenty-fifth anniversary at Lancaster. It is clear to me that God's hand has been upon you and your ministry there in a very special way. In every generation, God raises up certain men to make a difference and lead others. I believe that God has so used you. Your excellent spirit and your wise leadership have made a mark across this nation for the cause of Christ.

I also thank you for educating my fine assistant, Steve King, through the ministry of West Coast Baptist College. He has been a blessing to us and is doing a good job here.

May the Lord continue to richly bless you there as we serve Him together in this needy day and age. And, may I remain

a friend in Christ,

Dr. David Sorenson,
Pastor,
Northstar Baptist Church.

*A Lighthouse in The Northland*

# ✝✝✝ CALVARY
## life begins at Calvary Baptist Church

Dear Pastor Chappell and the members of Lancaster Baptist Church,

It is with great joy I congratulate you on twenty five years of ministry there in the Antelope Valley. Only eternity will reveal all that you folks have done in the lives of thousands not only there, but literally around the world. Thank you for your steadfastness and longevity to the old paths for Jesus Christ. God has used you and your ministry to inspire us to do more for the Lord Jesus Christ.

The annual Leadership Conference does so many things for the attendees from the preaching, the workshops, the music, and the vision of what can be done in our communities. Each time I come onto the campus of Lancaster Baptist Church, the Lord reminds me of what He can do for us. Your church vision is a tremendous encouragement to the countless thousands of pastors around the world.

Thank you also for having a vision for West Coast Baptist College. There are great sacrifices to start and sustain a college. Thank you for your sacrifice. It is a tremendous blessing to have a place of training in a distinguished church setting where we can send our young people. May God continue to use you, the ministry of Lancaster Baptist Church, and West Coast Baptist College. Keep the banner high for His name's sake. Be assured of our love and continued prayers for your ministry. May God give you many more years of Godly service.

Again, congratulations.

Yours for souls,

*Rick Stonestreet*

Pastor Rick Stonestreet

600 Gregory St., Fairfield, CA 94533 ● Phone (707) 422-7037 ● Fax (707) 422-3717 ● www.cbcf.net

# CALVARY BAPTIST CHURCH

210 Davis Road · Ashland OH 44805 · 419-281-0641 · www.cbcashland.org
Harry Strachan , Pastor

January 11, 2011

Dr. Paul Chappell
Lancaster Baptist Church
4020 E. Lancaster Blvd.
Lancaster, CA 93535

Dr. Chappell:

It is with great joy that I congratulate you on the 25 years of ministry at the Lancaster Baptist Church. Your vision and dedication to the cause of Christ and your desire for the souls of men to come to Christ has been an example and blessing to pastors and churches in America and around the world. Thank you for being a friend to pastors in helping them reach their communities for Christ and in enhancing their ministries with the right "tools" for such a time as this.

May god continue to bless you, your family and ministry with many more fruitful years.

God bless,

Harry Strachan
Pastor

January 26, 2011

Pastor Paul Chappell
4020 E. Lancaster Blvd.
Lancaster, CA 93535

Pastor Chappell,

Congratulations on twenty-five years of faithful ministry. It is truly amazing to see how the Lord has used you and the people of Lancaster Baptist Church over the years. Thank you for your un-wavering stand for right, your example of excellence, and your willingness to help resource ministries around the country. The people of Lighthouse Baptist Church and I congratulate you on this momentous occasion and wish twenty-five more years for you and your church family.

Sincerely,

Pastor Randy Tewell
RT/jt

Lighthouse Baptist Church | Pastor Randy Tewell
6905 Nan Gray Davis Road | Theodore, AL 36582 | 251.653.6542 | www.lbctheodore.com

# CENTRAL VALLEY BAPTIST CHURCH

*"More and More"*
*2011*

February 14, 2011

Pastor Paul Chappell
Lancaster Baptist Church
4020 E. Lancaster Blvd
Lancaster, CA 93535

Brother Chappell,

My ministry legacy is mostly in New England, only recently here in California. I very well recall hearing of the new work in Lancaster that had the touch of God upon it. It has been a real joy to not only have spent some time with you but to also have had the great privilege of preaching in your beautiful auditorium for college chapel.

Thank you friend, for your love for the local church and for men of God.

May the dear Lord continue His smile upon you and your excellent family. Congratulation on 25 years!

Pastor Eric M. Tharp
*Lan. 3:22,23*

Pastor Eric M. Tharp

ET:mj

10948 S. AIRPORT WAY     **PASTOR ERIC M. THARP**     MANTECA, CA 95336

PHONE (209) 982-9888     FAX (209) 983-0768     WWW.CVBCMANTECA.ORG

# Bay View Baptist Church

22648 Grosenbach Road  Washington, IL 61571

www.BayViewBaptistMinistries.org ♦ (309) 698-2000 PHONE ♦ (309) 698-2065 FAX

Dr. Keith D. Thibo
*Pastor*

January 13, 2011

Dr. Paul Chappell
Lancaster Baptist Church
4020 E. Lancaster Blvd.
Lancaster, CA 93535

Dear Dr. Chappell,

Congratulations on your twenty-five years at Lancaster Baptist Church. God has done a marvelous work through you, your family, your staff, and your church people. Every time I visit the church or the campus, I am spiritually refreshed and energized. Thank you for your national leadership and influence.

On a personal note, you are my dear and trusted friend. I wish we had met many years earlier. Your influence, example, and counsel have enhanced my personal spiritual life and the success of my work here. Thank you for being a pastor to pastors.

God bless you on this special day. May the celebration of twenty-five years bring rejoicing, as well as a fresh, new vision for the future.

Sincerely Serving,

Keith D. Thibo
Pastor

Illinois Central Christian School ♦ Morgan Street Chapel ♦ King's Kids International Baptist Mission

DWIGHT TOMLINSON

Dear Brother Chappell,

Gayle and I want to congratulate you and Terrie on 25 years of faithful and fruitful ministry in Lancaster. Who would have known 25 years ago that your influence would grow to be worldwide!

We consider it a great honor to count your family as dear friends. Our family has benefited greatly as God has touched us through your family.

We love you dearly and pray that our Lord will continue to pour out His blessings upon you.

Your Friend,

Dwight Tomlinson

*"...by love serve one another." Galatians 5:13*

LIBERTY BAPTIST CHURCH · 1000 BISON AVENUE · NEWPORT BEACH, CALIFORNIA 92660

# Dr. Jack Trieber

3530 DE LA CRUZ BOULEVARD
SANTA CLARA, CALIFORNIA 95054

February 8, 2011

Dr. & Mrs. Paul Chappell
Lancaster Baptist Church
4020 E. Lancaster Blvd.
Lancaster CA 93535

Dear Dr. and Mrs. Chappell,

What has transpired in the ministry of the Lancaster Baptist Church over the past twenty-five years is the exemplification of what God can accomplish through wholly yielded vessels. Your remarkable lives are a testimony for Christian laborers around the world of the Lord's goodness and faithfulness, proving true that He *"is able to do exceeding abundantly above all that we ask or think."* Thank you for dedicating yourselves to each other, to your family, and to the cause of Christ.

We would also like to express our gratefulness for the church family of Lancaster Baptist Church. Thank you for loving your pastor, his wife, and their family. The heartbeat of Dr. Chappell has surely found an echo in your dedication and faithful service; consequently, as pastor and people, you have accomplished much together for the Lord's work. The influence and reach of your church and West Coast Baptist College is felt across the nation and around the world. Truly, *"This is the LORD's doing; it is marvellous in our eyes."*

Thank you for being an encouragement to Mrs. Trieber and me as well as to the people of the North Valley Baptist Church. We love you dearly and pray that our Lord's hand of power and blessing—the same hand that has guided you to this momentous occasion—will continue to rest upon your lives as you serve Him for another twenty-five years and more.

Your friends,

*Jack and Cindie Trieber*
*and the North Valley Baptist Church*

# Bible Baptist Church

Bible Baptist
Church

4190
Susquehanna Trail
North

York, PA 17404

Phone:
717.266.0892

Fax:
717.266.6718

Website:
www.bbcyork.com

Pastor:
Dr. Kevin E. Trout

January 19, 2011

Dear Brother Chappell,

Please allow me to congratulate you on twenty-five years of ministry at Lancaster Baptist Church.

I am honored to write and let you know how much I appreciate you and the great influence you and your ministry have had on my life.

I have attended the Spiritual Leadership conference on several occasions and, have received encouragement and inspirational guidance at each one.

When we entered our building program here at Bible Baptist Church, York PA, several years ago I came out to Lancaster Baptist Church and caught a great vision by seeing all that God had done through your leadership.

We thank the Lord for you and the influence and the impact you have had on preachers and churches across our country.

Most esteemed,

Brother Trout

## A  FAMILY  TO  BE  LOVED

the caring church

# Valley Forge Baptist

**Scott Wendal**
Senior Pastor

January 24, 2011

**Sam Aylestock**
Associate Pastor
Student Ministries

Mr. Tim Christoson
Lancaster Baptist Church
4020 E. Lancaster Blvd
Lancaster, CA  93535

**Lamar Eifert**
Associate Pastor
Counseling

Dear Pastor Chappell,

Congratulations on 25 wonderful years of ministry at Lancaster Baptist Church.

**Greg Joyner**
Associate Pastor
Young Families

Pastor Chappell, I want to thank you for your godly spirit, warm friendship, and Christ-like example.  Through your ministry, you have been a mentor to me and our staff.  God has used the model of the Lancaster Baptist Church Family to multiply the Lord's work around the country and around the world.

**Ron Coulton**
Associate Pastor
Seniors

I also want to thank you for allowing the Lord use you to raise up WCBC for such a time as this.  We send you our students from across the country and you are sending them back to us four years later better than when you received them.  I want to thank the staff and church family for the great care of our students.  Nowhere in the country are college students treated in such a personable way.  All glory to God!

May God richly bless you with another 25 wonderful years in Lancaster.

Delighted to Serve,

Scott Wendal
Sr. Pastor
Valley Forge Baptist Temple

www.vfbt.org | 610.948.8100 | info@vfbt.org

616 S. Trappe Rd., Collegeville, PA 19426

# MISSIONARIES
# & FRIENDS FROM
# AROUND THE WORLD

**GREATER VANCOUVER**
**BAPTIST** CHURCH

15 February 2011

Dr Paul Chappell
Lancaster Baptist Church
4020 E Lancaster Blvd
Lancaster CA 93535

Dear Bro & Mrs Chappell,

I want to congratulate you on this wonderful milestone of your ministry. A quarter century of God's sustaining grace is truly a blessing to celebrate! It has been exciting to see the hand of God at work in miraculous ways through the years I have known you and I rejoice with you in all that God has done. I believe that in Pastor & Mrs Paul Chappell, God has found willing vessels that He has been able to use to impact the lives of thousands of people for the cause of Jesus Christ. Thank you for surrendering your lives to be used of God.

I am so thankful to the Lord for His allowing our paths to cross some thirteen years ago. My "ministry" life has been enriched and challenged to keep pressing on to make a difference. I have received much help through the various "Striving" ministries that has enable me to be a better pastor and overseer of the work God has given me. Many ideas and practical tips have made their way up the coast to find great usefulness here in Vancouver. Thanks for your vision help guys like me and for your willingness to share so much of yourself and your staff with us.

I have also been blessed in my "personal" life as well. Your friendship to me in difficult times has meant more than you can imagine. I have also been challenged and helped by your consistent spirit and attitude in the things of the Lord. You have always shown grace under fire and a determination to not allow things or people pull you away from the main thing. Thanks for being an example of God's power and grace to me.

Again, on behalf of our church family, the many students to have received their training at WCBC, and Josselyn and myself, we wish you God's very best in this year of celebration. Rest assured of our ongoing prayers for you, Terri and the ministry of LBC. May the Lord continue to keep His mighty hand upon you.

By His grace,

Gordon Conner
Pastor

*loving God  loving others*

4440 Victoria Drive | **Vancouver** | British Columbia | V5N 4NG | 604 874 7400 | **gvbc.ca**

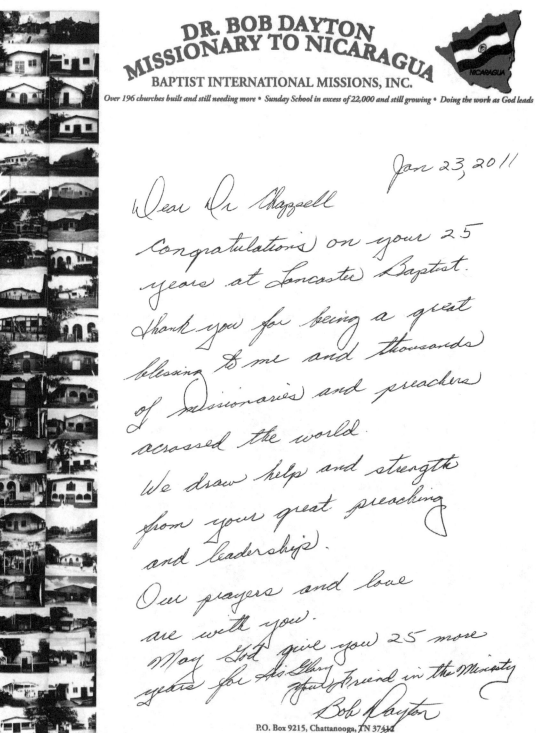

# DR. BOB DAYTON
## MISSIONARY TO NICARAGUA
### BAPTIST INTERNATIONAL MISSIONS, INC.

*Over 196 churches built and still needing more • Sunday School in excess of 22,000 and still growing • Doing the work as God leads*

Jan 23, 2011

Dear Dr Chappell

Congratulations on your 25 years at Lancaster Baptist. Thank you for being a great blessing to me and thousands of Missionaries and preachers acrossed the world.

We draw help and strength from your great preaching and leadership.

Our prayers and love are with you.

May God give you 25 more years for His Glory

Your Friend in the Ministry

Bob Dayton

P.O. Box 9215, Chattanooga, TN 37412
Home Phone: (864) 859-2799 • Email: Robertbimi@cs.com • Mission Phone: (423) 344-5050 • FAX: (423) 344-4774

**Baptist International Missions, Inc.**
P.O. Box 9215, Chattanooga, TN 37412, (423) 344-5050

**Leslie M. Frazier**
International Representative

January 18, 2011

Dr. Paul Chappell
Lancaster Baptist Church
4020 E. Lancaster Blvd.
Lancaster, CA 93535

Dear Dr. Chappell:

Congratulations on your 25th Church Anniversary. You have conspicuously met a need both in the ministry of your church and the West Coast Baptist College. Few have seen such growth as you have in these two areas. I believe it was David Hesselgrave who said:

*If you want to grow something to last a season—plant flowers.*
*If you want to grow something to last a lifetime—plant trees.*
*If you want to grow something to last through eternity—plant churches.*

Then we might add, if you want to meet the need of a lost world, train Gospel preachers. You are doing this. May the Lord give you strength and many more years in this great endeavor.

Sincerely in Christ,

Leslie M. Frazier
Far East Director

LF:ed

*Serving our Generation ... Reaching the Next*

*J. B. Godfrey*
*Far East Director*

January 11, 2011

Dr. Paul Chappell
4020 E. Lancaster Blvd.
Lancaster, CA 93535

Dear Dr. Chappell,

Some men have swayed a neighborhood or maybe even a town. Fewer have stirred a state and fewer still a region or a country. God has used you, your family, and your ministry to influence the world. People and places touched by the ministries of Lancaster Baptist Church are not just in Lancaster, nor in California, nor in the United States. Men and women, communities and countries all across the globe have been changed by those who have taken the message and example learned at Lancaster Baptist Church and West Coast Baptist College with them.

The emphasis on soul winning, the priority of the local church, biblical preaching and teaching, godly families, personal and ecclesiastical separation, encouraging God's people, loving God's preachers and their families, inspiring music, and being a pastor to your flock are among the reasons God has used you. The passion for souls, not only to win them but to disciple and encourage them, has spread under your leadership.

I thank the Lord and congratulate you, your wife, your family, and Lancaster Baptist Church for twenty-five years of manifesting the power and love of God. I pray that your godliness, faith, faithfulness, balance, and ability to find good men and women to help you will continue in the years ahead.  Many people will say with me, "There was a man sent from God."

Sincerely,

J.B. Godfrey

BAPTIST INTERNATIONAL MISSIONS, INC.

Mission Office: P. O. Box 9215 • Chattanooga, TN 37412 • Phone: 423 344 5050
Personal Office: 107 Chestnut St, Landrum, SC 29356 • Phone: 864 457 2047
E-mail: fareast@bimi.org

# MILITARY MINISTRIES

January 20, 2011

Dr. Paul Chappell
Lancaster Baptist Church
4020 E Lancaster Blvd
Lancaster CA 93535

Dear Dr. Chappell:

Gail and I would like to take this opportunity and congratulate you on 25 years of great service at Lancaster Baptist Church. I am so thrilled when I see the great work that is being done through Lancaster Baptist. Also we are highly impressed with the ministry of West Coast Baptist College and we do what we can to promote the school, especially in our military community.

Your church has the most balanced ministry of any church I have seen. May God richly bless the continued work of Lancaster Baptist Church.

Yours for Service Personnel,

James V. Kennard
II Timothy 2:2

JVK:flb

**Dr. James Kennard**
Director of Military Ministries
423-432-4898 • JKENNARDBIMI@CS.COM

**Dr. Jeff Alverson**
Assistant Director of Military Ministries
423-593-7625 • ALVERSONJ@AOL.COM

BAPTIST INTERNATIONAL MISSIONS, INC.
P.O. BOX 9215
CHATTANOOGA, TN 37412
(423) 344 5050

# BIBLE BAPTIST CHURCH

### Dr. Daniel Wooseang Kim. Pastor

### http://www.bkdbbc.org

242-3, Bul Kwang Dong, Eun Pyeng Gu, Seoul, 122-856 Korea
Tel:82-2-359-0559,355-7887  Fax:82-2-358-0110
E-mail : bbchurch@chollian.net
kim38110@chollian.net

## On the 25<sup>th</sup> Anniversary of Lancaster Baptist Church

Dear Dr. Paul Chappell,

Greetings from Seoul, Korea in the wonderful Name of our Lord Jesus Christ!

When I first came to the United States, the first home I stayed in was your father, Dr. Larry Chappell's, home. That was when I met you, in July 1967, and you were about six or seven years old then.  I still remember that you wanted to witness to one of your friends in your neighborhood, and you brought him over to me.  I presented the Gospel and won him for the Lord that day.  I couldn't help but notice that even though you were young, you had influence and a heart for winning souls.

Later your father came to Korea as a missionary, and you attended Seoul Foreign School.  While you were in high school, you attended our church occasionally, and you had already begun to preach that time.

As the Lord led you to Lancaster, CA, to start a church, I saw every stage of growth your church went through and how God blessed and used you in winning so many souls personally in your community.  Your ministry grew, not only in the community, but throughout the United States and eventually extended worldwide.  You raised so many fundamental preachers and ministers and sent them out as pastors, missionaries, and church workers who are well-trained and efficient in ministry.  I strongly believe that God raised you up for this generation.

Your godly influence also reached Korea, and many churches and pastors were challenged and encouraged by your ministry.  Especially, my son-in-law and my daughter are being trained under your leadership, and it is such a privilege for me to see them grow and be equipped.

And let us not be weary in well doing: for in due season we shall reap, if we faint not.  Galatians 6:9

# BIBLE BAPTIST CHURCH

### Dr. Daniel Wooseang Kim. Pastor

### http://www.bkdbbc.org

242-3, Bul Kwang Dong, Eun Pyeng Gu, Seoul, 122-856 Korea
Tel:82-2-359-0559,355-7887  Fax:82-2-358-0110
E-mail : bbchurch@chollian.net
kim38110@chollian.net

Surely, God has used you to influence so many around the world for the Gospel's sake.  As you celebrate the 25<sup>th</sup> Silver Anniversary of your church, the people of BulKwangDong Bible Baptist Church and I congratulate you with our whole heart. We send our love and rejoice with you on this very special occasion.  May God bless you for another 25 years, and more, to be used efficiently to win people in your community and worldwide and to train more people at West Coast Baptist College to start churches for His Great Commission!

Because of Calvary's love,

Daniel Wooseang Kim, D.D., Hum.D.
*Senior Pastor, BulKwangDong Bible Baptist Church*

---

And let us not be weary in well doing: for in due season we shall reap, if we faint not.   Galatians 6:9

# CHRISTIAN BIBLE BAPTIST CHURCH

Blk. 2 Lot 6-8 St. Francis Homes 2, Landayan, San Pedro, Laguna 4023
Website: www.cbbcphilippines.org   Email: info@cbbcphilippines.org
Tel: (02) 869-0433   Cel: (+63905) 300-4422   Dr. Ed Laurena - Pastor

**32** years of **GOD'S FAITHFULNESS**

February 15, 2011

Dr. Paul Chappell
4020 E. Lancaster Blvd.
Lancaster, CA 93535

Dear Pastor Chappell,

On behalf of Christian Bible Baptist Church, I would like to sincerely congratulate you on your 25$^{th}$ Church Anniversary.

I thank God for your example as good minister of our Lord and Saviour Jesus Christ, your powerful preaching, and soulwinning fervency. May God continue to use you, your supportive wife, and dedicated family in the ministry through Lancaster Baptist Church.

We in the Philippines, as well as the members of Christian Bible Baptist Church-San Pedro, Laguna, greatly admire your faithfulness. I want you to know that you are a great influence to all servant-leaders, especially to me.

Please accept my heartiest congratulations to your accomplishments in His ministry!

For the lost souls,

Pastor Ed Laurena

Soulwinning | 7-Stage Discipleship | Sunday School | Bus and Jeepney | Foreign & Local Missions | Outreaches
Baptist Heritage Bible College | Christian Bible Baptist Academy | School for the Deaf
Moral Recovery Program | Loving Hands Orphanage | Heritage Publications

**THE MARTINS**
Your Missionaries in the Philippines

Dear Brother Chappell:

Becky and I would like to congratulate you and Mrs. Chappell, as well as your church family, on your 25th anniversary! I'm sure this is a very exciting time for you, as you look back through the years at all the precious memories. Serving the Lord is the greatest "job" on earth isn't it?

Iloilo Baptist Church loves you and the Lancaster Baptist Church very much. We have thoroughly enjoyed it every time you have sent a visitor our way. They have always been a blessing.

We will never forget the times you have helped us in times of trouble—like when we had the fire, that burned down our dorm and staff houses, and the terrible typhoon that killed so many people and destroyed so many of our graduates' churches. I could never properly express my gratitude for your friendship. If a person went their whole life and had only one friend like you, they would be most blessed. Striving together with you for the 14 years I have known you has encouraged my heart.

Mrs. Chappell, thank you so much for being such an outstanding pastors' wife. Thank you for raising such godly children.

Thank God for a church and Bible college like yours that has a passion for lost souls, both in your region, for our country, and around the world as you continue to support and send out missionaries. Thank you, Brother and Mrs. Chappell, for having the strength of character and courage not to quit when things got tough.

God bless you!

Sincerely in Christ,

Rick Martin

FIELD ADDRESS:
P.O Box 88, Iloilo City, Philippines 5000
Tel # (63-33) 3204557
Fax # (63-33) 3203677

MISSION ADDRESS:
Baptist International Missions, Inc.
Box 9215, Chattanooga, Tn 37412

HOME ADDRESS:
1899 Saddleback Blvd., #4
Norman OK 73072, USA
405-329-8515

**Senri Newtown**
**Baptist Church**
3-11-32 Imamiya
Mino-city Osaka 562-0033 Japan
Phone:072.726.0726
Fax:072.726.0276
E-mail office@senrinewtown.com
URL http://www.senrinewtown.com

February 8, 2011

Dr. and Mrs. Paul Chappell
Lancaster Baptist Church
4020 E. Lancaster Blvd.
Lancaster, CA 93535

Dear Dr. and Mrs. Paul Chappell

Congratulations on your 25th Anniversary of ministry.

I praise the Lord for His many wonderful blessings upon your faithful ministry in Lancaster CA. I had heard much about you from American pastors and missionaries in Japan. But when I first visited your church through the introduction of Dr. Don Sisk in 2003, I was much impressed by your ministry. I praise the Lord for your passion for souls and your sacrificial works and growing ministry there.

You must have had many trials that nobody knows for these 25 years.
     25 years of prayer and sermon preparation
     25 years of soulwinnig
     25 years of counseling
     25 years of facing the congregation
     25 years of waiting on God
     25 years of seeking His perfect will
     25 years of working with your staff
     25 years of fighting Satan
     25 years of problems
     25 years of heartaches
You have had all of this and more. I know as a pastor that you shed tears for difficulties many times, but you have been greatly used of God.

Mrs.Ogawa and I will never forget your more than generous hospitality at your church, your house and the hotel. It is my prayer that God will give you 25 more years (if the Lord tarries His coming) to proclaim the unsearchable riches of Christ.

May the Lord bless you in a special way.

In Him,

*Sogoro Ogawa*

Sogoro Ogawa, Pastor
Senri Newtown Baptist Church
Osaka, Japan

**SENRI NEWTOWN**
BAPTIST CHURCH

**BIMI** BAPTIST INTERNATIONAL MISSIONS, INC.

**James Ray**
**International Representative**
100+ Nations Ministry
International Bible Ministry

January 20, 2011

Dr. Paul Chappell
Lancaster Baptist Church
5020 E Lancaster Blvd
Lancaster CA 93535

Dear Dr. Chappell:

Mary and I, along with our co-workers at Baptist International Missions, would like
to congratulate you on the wonderful achievement of 25 years with Lancaster Baptist
Church. There are events in every generation that highlight in a special way the
working of God. Lancaster Baptist Church and the ministry God has given to you
and your wife certainly would be one of these highlights. It has been amazing for all
of us to see the hand of God in the ministry of West Coast Baptist College and
Lancaster Baptist Church. Every great work, however, has a human face and human
involvement. Your sacrifice and faithfulness in the task to which God has called you
is an example to all of us.

We thank God for you and that He has brought you to the kingdom for such a time as
this. Our prayers continue for you as you continue the great work to which God has
called you. Thank you for being an example as well as a friend to all of us.

I am...

Yours for the harvest,

James R. Ray
BIMI
Psalm 27:1

JRR:flb

PO Box 9215
Chattanooga TN 37412
Phone: 423 344 5050
Fax: 423 344 4774
www.bimi.org

Dr Wayne Sehmish
Serving in Thailand

10th February, 2011

Dear Bro. Chappell,

Congratulations on twenty five years of ministry with the people of Lancaster Baptist Church. The Glory is the Lords for the great things He has done amongst you there.

I am certain the story of these years is the story of thousands coming to Christ and an untold number of lives changed through your faithfulness in heeding the Lord's call to come to Lancaster, and your faithfulness in serving Him over these past twenty five years.

Your preaching has been without fear or favor and God's Spirit upon you is clear for all to see. Only God knows how many life-changing, family-changing decisions have been made as people have heard you plainly declare forth God's Word from the pulpit of the Lancaster Baptist Church and abroad.

Your faithfulness and good hand of God upon the Lancaster Baptist Church has encouraged and strengthened others to stay at their own works all over the world. You have been a voice of balance and reason in fundamentalism that has been a light to many of us. You have boldly stood your ground, but you have always stood on the Word of God. I truly thank God for raising you up for the hour we minister in. Making God the goal and not growth has not just been a slogan, it is the explanation for what we all see at the Lancaster Baptist Church.

God bless you Bro. Chappell, may His grace and His strength be your unending portion for all that His will has for you in the future. Thank you for your friendship to God's men all over the world.

Yours sincerely,

Wayne Sehmish.

| American Contact/Support | Sending Church/Australian Support | Address in Thailand |
| --- | --- | --- |
| Lighthouse Baptist Church | Good Shepherd Baptist Church | APT 110, 15th Floor |
| 1345 Skyline Drive | 185 Old Northern Road | St Louis Grand Terrace |
| Lemon Grove, CA 91945 | Albany Creek, Queensland | Soi St Louis, Sth Sathorn Road |
| | Australia 4035 | Yanawa, Sathorn |
| | | Bangkok, Thailand 10120 |
| | | drwayne@baptist.com.au |

www.thesimpletruth.com.au

**BAPTIST INTERNATIONAL MISSIONS, INC.**

*Dr. Don Sisk, General Director Emeritus*

February 10, 2011

Dr. Paul Chappell
Lancaster Baptist Church
4020 E. Lancaster Blvd.
Lancaster, CA 93535

Dear Dr. Chappell:

Congratulations on 25 years of faithful and fruitful service at Lancaster Baptist Church! The past 25 years have been a story of unparalleled growth for Lancaster Baptist Church. I have watched with much interest and prayers as I followed the progress of this great ministry.

When I was invited to come and preach at Lancaster Baptist some 20 years ago, I had no idea how much that developing relationship with you and the church would impact my life. It has been my great privilege to observe closely the great work that God has done through the Lancaster Baptist Church. I have watched the great numerical growth of the church and have observed the great influence that God has granted this ministry. People all over the world are looking toward this place for encouragement, enlightenment and information.

I believe that Lancaster Baptist Church has become a great model for other churches because of its multifaceted ministry. Glorifying God is the basis for everything that you have done. Servant leadership has been preached and practiced by the pastor and other leaders of the church. Soul winning has been kept at the center of the ministry and has produced thousands of people who will be in Heaven worshiping God for eternity. A great emphasis on discipleship has resulted in hundreds of mature believers who are reproducing other believers and other leaders. The impact on the Antelope Valley has been nothing short of miraculous.

The unselfish attitude of you, Pastor Chappell, and the members of the Lancaster Baptist is manifested in your willingness to unselfishly give of yourself and your means to help other churches. The thing that I have been impressed with perhaps more than anything else is your great worldwide vision. Your great emphasis on world missions has resulted in millions of dollars given to evangelize the world. West Coast Baptist College is training future leaders for the churches of America and missionaries for the world. The phenomenal growth of the college is evidence of God's blessings.

For the past ten years it has been a great joy for Virginia and me to be members of this great church. Thank you for allowing us to share with you. Our lives have been enriched because of you and the church. We love you and appreciate you and your dear wife more than mere words could express. Our prayer is that God will keep you in the center of His great hand and continue to *bless* and *use* you.

Yours because of Him,

Don Sisk Ps.126:5.6

Don Sisk

PO Box 9215
Chattanooga TN 37412
Phone: 423 344 5050
Fax: 423 344 4774
www.bimi.org

DS:ed

88

# BIMI BAPTIST INTERNATIONAL MISSIONS, INC.

### DR. DAVID SNYDER PRESIDENT & GENERAL DIRECTOR

January 14, 2011

Dr. Paul Chappell
Lancaster Baptist Church
4020 E. Lancaster Blvd.
Lancaster, CA 93535

Dear Dr. Chappell,

Greetings from BIMI's World Missions Center. I am writing to say "Congratulations" on 25 years of ministry!

We rejoice with you in what God has done through your ministry there in Lancaster. I know of many lives that have been impacted by Lancaster Baptist Church, West Coast Baptist College, and Striving Together Publications. It is wonderful to know that your church is truly having a worldwide impact.

Additionally, I am very grateful for your many years of service as a trustee of Baptist International Missions, Inc. Your contribution here has been tremendous. I thank you for taking time out of your schedule to come to Chattanooga for our Board meetings and for the many other ways you have assisted us in our ministry.

Again, Congratulations! We praise the Lord with you for 25 incredible years of ministry. May the LORD richly bless you.

In Christ,

David H. Snyder
John 15:16

DHS:ljb

PO Box 9215
Chattanooga TN 37412
Phone: 423 344 5050
Fax: 423 344 4774
www.bimi.org

# OTHERS SERVANTS OF GOD

www.baydo.com

Dear Pastor Chappell,

I would first like to applaud you for twenty-five years of ministry. God has accomplished so much through you, only because you dedicated your life and your all to Jesus Christ. You have never let fear stop you from moving forward for the cause of Christ. You have surrounded yourself with good, godly people. You pray, study, and seek wise counsel before moving forward on any project only wanting the best for your church family. God has given you the ability to become a great leader, but I know it has come at a great cost. I know there have been hours upon hours of studying on how to be a better leader. But above all, you have never put your family aside. The love that you show your wife and children and what they mean to you by taking time for them is commendable. I personally want to thank you and your church family for the love and concern you have shown my family and me. Thank you for your friendship. Congratulations on a job well done.

Your Brother in Christ,

Ernie Baydo
Roy, WA

35108 92ND AVE. S. ☛ P.O. BOX 1410 ☛ MCKENNA, WA 98558 ☛ OFFICE: 360-400-2438 ☛ FAX: 360-400-0738

www.baydo.com

January 18, 2011

Pastor Chappell,

Congratulations to you, your staff and church family and a huge "thank you" to our Lord for 25 years of amazing accomplishments. It is amazing what God is doing with your ministry. You are truly making a difference in so many lives and ministries. I know God must be exceeding way beyond what you could have imagined when you first stood on that corner 25 years ago. Isn't it wonderful what He can do with a soul sold out for him?

Paul, I just want to say, from the very moment I first met you, you have been so full of grace towards me. Thank you for that. Your fervent service to our Lord and the amazing talents of leadership He has blessed you with is a major source of encouragement and motivation for me to be a better Christian man. You inspire me with your preaching, your writings, your friendship and most of all, the example of your Christian walk.

It is exciting times to be alive and to see how the Lord is working just prior to His return, but if the Lord tarries, I can only imagine what the next 25 years will bring. If there is anything I can do to be of service to you, my brother, please call on me.

Love in the Lord,

Walt Baydo

35108 92ND AVE. S. ◆ P.O. BOX 1410 ◆ MCKENNA, WA 98558 ◆ OFFICE: 360-400-2438 ◆ FAX: 360-400-0738

January 12, 2011

Dear Dr. Chappell,

It is with great joy and honor that I can contribute to this great anniversary for you on this occasion. You deserve the utmost respect and congratulations for your faithfulness to the calling of God. God only knows how many others besides me you have greatly influenced for good and God. You have presented to us all what a godly and balanced ministry looks like. I thank you so much for your friendship and partnership in this great battle we Christians face. It is good to know we have you in our trenches.

God is so good,

Bro. John Bishop

John and Donna Bishop

99 Christian Ranch Road • Rose Bud, Arkansas 72137 • 501.556.5837 • www.godissogood.net

A Ministry of Franklin Road Baptist Church

3148 Franklin Road • Murfreesboro, TN 37128 • 615.890.0820 • Dr. Mike Norris, Pastor

# Franklin Road
## BAPTIST CHURCH
*Ministries*

*Dr. Mike Norris, Pastor*

January 12, 2011

Dr. Paul Chappell
Lancaster Baptist Church
4010 E. Lancaster Blvd.
Lancaster, CA 93535

Dear Dr. Paul Chappell,

Our society has taught the younger generation to find hero's in life and to pattern themselves after those hero's. Unfortunately, the hero's that most choose to follow do not honor God with their life. As a younger preacher, I have sought diligently and watched carefully who I want to emulate. There are few that I would call my "hero."

Dr. Chappell, your walk with God is evident; not in the size of your ministry, but rather in how you treat the "least of these." You have always treated me so kindly even before we officially met. You have taught me by your example to love everybody - no matter the prestige or name. It is no wonder that God has blessed your ministry in such great ways! Thank you for not only being a "preacher," but also a "Pastor" with a heart to make a difference for God all across our world.

I love you and I pray daily for you. May God grant you another twenty five years of impacting our world for Christ!

Your Friend,

*Kurt Copeland*

Kurt Copeland
Youth Pastor
Franklin Road Baptist Church
Isaiah 6:8

---

3148 FRANKLIN ROAD ◆ MURFREESBORO, TN 37128 ◆ 615.890.0820 ◆ 615.890.0821 fax ◆ www.frbc.com

February 3, 20011

Brother Chappell,

It is not often that we have the opportunity to send our best wishes on such a momentous occasion as this. For a preacher to remain so committed to his call and calling as you have for these many years is becoming all too rare. Milestones such as this mark our time here on this earth as either being divinely profitable or as being wasted with opportunity lost. We are so very happy for you and your family. It is indeed a special time to commemorate. Twenty-five years of faithful service in one place is no small matter. I know that Lancaster Baptist Church is very proud to have you as their pastor and rightfully so. God has used you and the wonderful people of LBC in such a marvelous way over the years. I hope they understand what a blessing they have been to so many of us who consider them and you our friend and fellow servants in Christ.

Years ago I remember visiting your very young church there in Lancaster and listening to you preach on a summer's evening service. LBC even in those days was a special place to visit and it was obvious that God had given their young pastor a tremendous vision not to mention the necessary gifts to bring that vision to pass. I later said to my wife, Marilyn, that I believed God was going to do great things in that place and certainly, God has done just that. Little did I know at that time that one day my own children, Ryan, Matthew and Amber would be trained and guided under your leadership and influence at WCBC. Many hundreds of other parents, I know, could say the same thing.

Sir, we are indebted to you and the God we serve! As Daniel of old said, "There is a God in heaven" and He directs the affairs of men if they will let Him. We are thankful that God's good hand has been upon you and we pray it may continue for many years to come to God's honor and glory.

I am privileged to consider you a friend. Thank you for your kindness, your wise counsel and encouragement at times when it was needed and much appreciated. We trust that this time of remembrance will be a very special time for you, your dear family and the staff and members of the Lancaster Baptist Church.

To God be Glory
and Dominion Forever,

Brother Mike Gass
Harvest Baptist Temple

2001 S. Columbus Ave. Medford OR, 97501 • 541-773-3141 • Bob Gass, Pastor

# CHRISTIAN LAW ASSOCIATION

*A Ministry of Helps to Bible-Believing Churches and Christians*

Dear Pastor and Mrs. Chappell:

It is a wonderful honor for me to be able to congratulate you on your 25th anniversary year of service at the Lancaster Baptist Church. It is with my most heartfelt and sincere words of appreciation and thankfulness that I express my gratitude for how you have allowed the Lord to use you to do such a mighty outreach for the cause of Jesus Christ.

For 25 years, I have watched as you have faithfully served with distinction in the times of trial and testing, as well as in the times of glorious blessing and "mountain top" experiences. You have served with the same steadfast spirit of dedication to Jesus Christ no matter what seas of life the Lord has placed you in, and no matter who has befriended or assailed what the Lord has led you to accomplish. For 25 years, you have been the Lord's faithful servants and friends. For that, Pastor, I salute you and Mrs. Chappell with great fervency. Well done, well done, well done!

While the accomplishments of your ministry have been stellar and nothing short of amazing, it is the heart and spirit that you have maintained in yourselves, your family, and your people that is the most glorious of accomplishments by far.

For 25 years, you have shown us how to love the Lord and how to love and reach people for the Lord's honor and glory! The buildings and projects that the Lord has led you to undertake in these years are fantastic and truly remarkable. But the spirit and heart that you have maintained, and then modeled and taught to others, is the true value of all of your accomplishments for the Lord. You have done great deeds with a great heart! You have not just shown us what to do, but you have shown us how to be all that the Bible commands us to be!

For 25 years, you have shouldered the heartaches and burdens of not just your own people, but also the burdens and heartaches of so many across America and around the world. I have watched as you have with broken hearts shed many tears for those who needed your counsel and prayers. Your tender hearts have remained unchanged since the first day, 25 years ago.

You have cared and loved the Lord and others so passionately – and nothing has changed that as the years have passed. As so many others would say, Pastor and Mrs. Chappell, I treasure your friendship. Your lives have profoundly touched my family, my ministry, and me.

We surely do thank the Lord for all of the magnificent things that you have accomplished. But most of all we are thankful for what and who you are. Your hearts and spirits are wonderful treasures of God's grace. Thank you for sharing that treasure for 25 years so faithfully. Thank you for so selflessly and graciously sharing yourselves for others. The greatest days of your lives and ministry, by promise of God, are in the future. Congratulations for the past truly fantastic 25 years! But thank you most of all for having the servant's heart that has touched our lives. Because of your lives, we will never be the same.

Praise the Lord for your 25 years of life-changing ministry!

Your thankful friend,

David C. Gibbs, Jr.

PO Box 4010 Seminole, FL 33775-4010
Ph 727.399.8300 | Fax 727.398.3907
www.christianlaw.org

**3883 HWY 49 SO.**
**MARIPOSA, CA 95338**

Dear Pastor Chappell,

Congratulations and thank you for being a faithful servant for the past twenty five years of your ministry at Lancaster Baptist Church. I have heard it said more than once that visiting your church and college property is as close as we can be to heaven here on earth. I personally feel the presence of the Lord each time I visit the church.

Thank you for being a friend and an encouragement to my family and me for the past thirteen years. Thank you for being a willing sacrifice, making up the hedge, and standing in the gap before our Lord. Because of the college and the church, our daughter was directly influenced, encouraged, and trained to serve the Lord and is now married to a faithful young man who is in full time ministry serving the Lord. Seeing how you influence so many lives throughout the United States and around the world is a blessing to me. Your hospitality and the giving of yourself to others on a consistent basis is a living example of how the Bible teaches us to love the Lord with all our heart, and to love others as ourselves. Thank you for the many letters and cards you have sent to me over the years. Thank you for all the godly books. All these many things have been a tremendous blessing to me.

My prayer is that the Lord will continue to give you the strength and zeal to serve Him for many years to come.

May God bless and keep you.

Your Brother in the Lord,

Ken Giorgi

**WEST COAST BAPTIST COLLEGE**

*Training Laborers for His Harvest*

*July 2011*

*Pastor and Mrs. Terri Chappell*
*Lancaster Baptist Church*
*4020 E. Lancaster Blvd.*
*Lancaster, CA 93535*

*Dear Pastor and Mrs. Chappell,*

*My heart still burns when I think back to my senior year of college as I sat in chapel and listened to your Dad preach about the great need in California. I had no idea at that time why God was planting those seeds of burden in my heart but now almost 40 years later the picture is much clearer. I never met your father that day but several years later when our paths crossed God had prepared me and my heart was immediately knit to your life and ministry.*

*I'm glad that God has all of the dots of our life connected in His perfect plan and I am grateful that the dots of your life and mine ran close enough together for us to share many times together in revival work. Now it is my joy simply to walk with you as you follow God's direction for Lancaster Baptist Church and West Coast Baptist College. Thank you for your love for God, your vision for ministry, your passion for revival, and your faithfulness to God's call in your life here in Lancaster for these twenty-five years.*

*I am praying that God will allow this anniversary to be filled with wonderful memories of God's provision and power and that it will encourage you to keep pressing forward until the trumpet sounds or God calls you home. Thank you for striving together with God and with us as a church family for the faith of the Gospel.*

*Love in Christ,*

*Dr. John Goetsch*

4010 E. Lancaster Blvd
Lancaster, CA 93535
888.694.9222
wcbc.edu
661.946.4510 fax
Dr. Paul Chappell, President

# Tim Green

1198 KASH DRIVE, DAY HEIGHTS, OHIO 45150   (513) 831-6050

January Eighteen
Two Thousand Eleven


Dr. Paul Chappell
Lancaster Baptist Church
4020 E. Lancaster Boulevard
Lancaster, California

Dear Bro. Paul,

In New Testament times Paul wrote to Timothy, however, the roles are reversed in our day. This minor Timothy is writing to a major Paul.

CONGRATULATIONS on your Twenty-fifth anniversary as pastor! I preached my dad's Fifty-fifth anniversary last August, so you have a ways to go! By the way, this Timothy will not be writing you three decades from now! I will be dwelling in my mansion and beholding the face of the One Who died for me and purchased my salvation on Calvary! Well, enough about me and Jesus.

One thousand and three hundred Sundays of sermons–Wow! Souls saved, baptized and discipled by the thousands; missionaries sent and students trained–God be praised! You have been a kind and thoughtful friend from my distant vantage point, and you have loved my sons and helped all three of them immensely. They love you, respect you and look up to you.

May God give you and Terrie many more wonderful years of service. Thirty? You never know!

In mine own hand,

Timothy Green

MAJESTY MUSIC. INC.

*Sacred Music You Can Trust*

February 18, 2011

Pastor Paul Chappell
4020 E. Lancaster Blvd.
Lancaster, CA 93535

Dear Brother Chappell,

Ahoy, mate! I sailed the Jolly Roger into port today so that I could send you a letter of congratulations on 25 years of ministry at Lancaster Baptist Church. How I appreciate the influence that you are having on churches across America and around the world.

Your emphasis on soul-winning, strong preaching, and faithfulness to God's Word is having a much-needed impact. Thank you for continuing to go forward for Christ and for providing a model of a church that is striving to fulfill the great commission.

Brother Chappell, I love you and I pray that God will give you many more years of ministry at the helm of LBC. Thank you for your friendship and your faithfulness.

Rejoicing in the Lord,

Ron *Patch* Hamilton
Phil. 4:4

733 Wade Hampton Blvd    Greenville, SC 29609    864-242-6722

# Dr. Raymond L. Hancock

Residence:
4412 Acoma Circle
Williamsburg, VA 23188
(757) 345-5885
Cell: (757) 561-4581

**January 15, 2011**

**Dear Dr. Chappell,**

**Congratulations to you, your family, and your church on the 25 years of dedicated service for our Lord Jesus. Greatness in life or work does not happen by accident. True greatness comes first by dedicated leadership and then dedicated followship. A people Coming Together is a Beginning, a people Staying Together is Progress, but a People Working Together is Success. The testimony of Coming Together, Staying Together and Working Together is evident in this day of celebration of 25 years of laboring together.**

**Dr. Chappell you have a unique quality that some men lack. While some can preach the whole truth and inspire the listeners, they fail to be able to motivate them to do a great work. Dr. Chappell you are truly a motivator which is so desperately needed. The evidence is seen in the many souls being saved and the training of the young to do the work of the ministry, and the great church in Lancaster.**

**You are a dear friend and I have always been blessed in my visits both in the church and in the college. I am sure this is a day of rejoicing for all, as you look at all the blessings of God upon the work there. You and your family have labored faithfully and our Lord will never forget your labor of love for Him. Only eternity will reveal all that has been done.**

**May you have a wonderful day, and may the Lord continue to bless you and yours is our prayer.**

**For Him and By Him,**
**I remain your friend for the journey,**

*Raymond Hancock*

**Raymond Hancock**

"It is not enough to care, you must care enough."

# Evangelist Hal Hightower

February 1, 2011

Dr. Paul Chappell
Lancaster Baptist Church
4020 E. Lancaster Blvd.
Lancaster CA 93535

Dear Bro. Chappell,

Congratulations on twenty five years of faithful and fruitful service at Lancaster Baptist Church. I am very thankful that the Lord has used your vision, hard work, and ministry to have an impact on our nation and our world in such a time as this.

Thank you for your friendship and thank you for your investment in others. I pray for you often and am thankful to call you a friend of mine. May God give you twenty five more years of much fruit.

For souls,

Hal Hightower

## From the Desk of Dr. Eldon Martens

January 27, 2011

Dear Pastor Chappell,

As I offer my congratulations on this 25th Anniversary I stand amazed at the dimension to which our Lord has blessed and used you.

I count it an honor to know you as a friend, fellow Pastor and now as my Pastor and a member of your staff.

Few men in history have been more greatly blessed. As you have walked with integrity and humility, the Lord has multiplied your ministry far beyond anything, I am sure, you even imagined. Your vision, work ethic and passion to reach the lost, build up the saints and lift up our Savior has brought about the model church of ministry in this key time of history.

Thank you for your faithfulness, statesmanship and vision that are an inspiration to all.

The greatest days are yet ahead, and by God's Grace I look forward to being a part of what the Lord will do.

Your Friend,

Brother Eldon Martens

2742 Fremont Avenue
Clovis, CA 93611
Cell – (559)259-1118
E-mail – docmart@juno.com

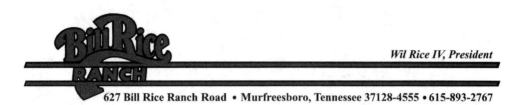

*Wil Rice IV, President*

**627 Bill Rice Ranch Road • Murfreesboro, Tennessee 37128-4555 • 615-893-2767**

April 19, 2011

Dr. Paul Chappell
Lancaster Baptist Church
4020 E. Lancaster Blvd.
Lancaster, CA 93535

Dear Brother Chappell,

Well, it is hard to believe that you are celebrating 25 years there at Lancaster Baptist. That is a wonderful achievement.

Recently, a young lady who works with us in the ministries here, flew out to California to see West Coast Baptist College. When Mary and I sent her a text asking what she thought of the school, she simply answered, "Wonderful!"

That was a blessing to us because she has been looking for a school for some months and praying about the possibility of getting into a Bible college. One brief visit answered all of her questions and prayers.

I suspect that has happened hundreds of times. And Mary and I are thankful for the leadership you have provided to Lancaster Baptist and to West Coast Baptist College. We believe the Lord has blessed there and is blessing the ministry. In a word, I would say, "wonderful!"

May the Lord bless you during this special time.

Your friend,

Bill Rice III

*"...the Deaf hear...the poor have the gospel preached to them."*

**WITH CHAD SCHEARER**

Bro. & Mrs. Chappell,

Congratulations on 25 years at Lancaster Baptist Church. What an accomplishment for the Lord! You are a true example of being a soldier for Christ. Over the years you have led your people on a journey of growth that continues to build each day. Lancaster Baptist Church has become a beacon of hope to a lost world. Your college is training up a generation of compassionate caring young people with a desire to reach the world. The Striving Together ministry has been such a blessing to so many who need resources to live and teach others about Christ. I have been using the Sunday School material for several years and it is always laid out so perfectly for people to understand.

Not only have we had the chance to spend time with you in Lancaster at your church and college but also in the hunting fields of Montana and Africa. Walker still talks about the time he came with me to Lancaster and the fun time he had. The man behind the pulpit is the same man in the field; A true example of a person whose steps are ordered by the Lord. We have enjoyed our time around the campfire.

You have also been an example of a Godly family man. Getting to know your family has been such a blessing to Marsha and me. Through your family you can definitely see the consistent influence you have had on their lives. Marsha has especially enjoyed the time she has had to get to know Mrs. Chappell.

Thank you for your friendship. We will continue to pray for you and your ministry and hope that the next 25 years will be greater yet.

Your friends,

Chad & Marsha Schearer

# Evangelist Paul Schwanke

38036 North 15th Avenue
Desert Hills, Arizona 85086
(623) 910-5747
www.preachthebible.com

January 10, 2011

Pastor and Mrs. Paul Chappell
Lancaster Baptist Church
4020 E Lancaster Blvd
Lancaster, CA 93535

Dear Brother and Mrs. Chappell,

Cathy and I wanted to join your church and friends around the world in congratulating you on your 25th anniversary at Lancaster Baptist Church. How thankful we are that you obeyed the call of God upon your lives years ago, and surrendered to serve Him. Only eternity will reveal the fruits of your tireless labors for Him.

We are thankful for your friendship and encouragement. Your love for Christ and also for people are a great inspiration. Brother Chappell, your faithful Bible preaching is a source of strength to far more than you will ever know this side of Heaven.

Should the Lord tarry His return, we trust the next 25 will be even more blessed than the past 25. Stay encouraged in the Lord.

Looking for the Blessed Hope,

Paul and Cathy Schwanke

*"Therefore, my beloved brethren, be ye stedfast, unmoveable,*
*always abounding in the work of the Lord,*
*forasmuch as ye know that your labour is not in vain in the Lord."*

*Preaching the Cross ... the Power of God*

# John and Marilyn Turner

1130 Grange Hall Rd. Milton, PA 17847
Tel: 570-742-2846   Cell: 570-490-6250   php31314@gmail.com

Dear Pastor Chappell,

As you and Lancaster Baptist Church celebrate twenty five years of ministry together I want to congratulate you and also thank you for being a "*vessel unto honour, sanctified, and meet for the master's use, and prepared unto every good work*". When I think of Lancaster Baptist Church and the character of the ministry, I think of "servant leadership". The reason that character permeates the ministry is that it permeates your character and then flows from your heart to the entire ministry. In the years that I have been associated with your ministry, I have on more than one occasion had a need met by one of the "servants" in your ministry, both staff and church members. I love church and the church that I love most outside of my home church is Lancaster Baptist Church.

One of the things I love most about Lancaster Baptist Church is your heart for souls. You reach thousands yearly with the Gospel and invested in discipling them to maturity as Christians. You have also had a heart to help other ministries do the same and therefor are a partner in reaching millions for Christ! I can say with certainty that souls have been reached by Bethel Baptist Church in Pennsylvania that would not have been reached were it not for the influence of your ministry.

You also have carried the mantle of fundamentalism into the 21st century as no one else has. You have preserved every tenet of the" fundamentals" while delivering the message in a way that is relevant to the day we live in. I believe that Lancaster Baptist Church is the model of the New Testament Church in the 21st century. My sons have been blessed to be trained in this ministry and I pray that they carry the lessons they learned there throughout their lives.

In closing I would like to say that I have been privileged to know you and am a better man for it.

Sincerely,

John F. Turner, MD, FACS

**Wallace Ministries** · **425 Sharondale Drive** · **Murfreesboro, TN  37129**
**Cell: (615) 394-5470** · **Home: (615) 890-1471**

**January 12, 2011**

**Dr. Paul Chappell**
**Lancaster Baptist Church**
**4020 E. Lancaster Blvd.**
**Lancaster, CA  93535**

**Dear Bro. Chappell,**

**My sincere CONGRATULATIONS to you and your family on the wonderful milestone of twenty-five years of witnessing the miracle of the ministries of Lancaster Baptist Church and West Coast Baptist College. Who would have imagined what God would do in and through the little boy I saw years ago when I preached for your dad at the First Baptist Church of Long Beach.**

**I have you in a place of priority on my morning prayer list and have prayed for you for many years. I plan to keep doing so. Thank you for your balance in the ministry and praise the Lord for the impact and influence on your city, the entire West coast, the nation, and around the world.**

**I am so glad when I come to visit your campus and occasionally in meetings around the country to see the Weavers and Rasmussen's. Both Rita and Susan  were playmates with my children at college in the early fifties.**

**I wish God's blessing on your anniversary week and wish I could be there to rejoice with you, however my schedule will prevent that. God bless you and Terry.**

**Sincerely yours,**

*Tom Wallace*

**Dr. Tom Wallace**

**Website: www.wallaceministries.com** · **E-Mail: thwallace@comcast.net**

# BUSINESSMEN

**ATKINSON AND ASSOCIATES, INC.**

GENERAL CONTRACTORS

LICENSE NO. 597362

233 EAST AVENUE K-6

LANCASTER, CALIFORNIA 93535

(661) 723-5141

(661) 723-3728 FAX

February 14, 2011

Pastor Chappell
Lancaster Baptist Church
4020 E. Lancaster Blvd.
Lancaster, CA 93535

Dear Pastor Chappell,

I just wanted to take a few moments of your time to congratulate you, upon Twenty-five years of a very successful church building ministry. We have been fortunate enough to be able to work with yourself and your team, to construct some of your buildings, to enable your ministry to continue to grow to this point and into the future.

Being aware of the churches humble bringing, to where the church is today, is beyond impressive. Under the Lord's guidance and your direction, Lancaster Baptist Church is not only a church, is a school for the lord from pre-school all the way through college.

We wish you continue success to being able to bring God's people to the Lord.

Sincerely,
**ATKINSON AND ASSOCIATES**

George B. Atkinson
President

# BICKEL UNDERWOOD

### JAMES S. BICKEL JR. ARCHITECT
## A CALIFORNIA CORPORATION

January 18, 2011

Pastor Paul Chappell
**Lancaster Baptist Church**
4020 E. Lancaster Blvd.
Lancaster, CA 93535

**Re:** Congratulations on 25 years!

Dear Pastor Chappell,

It is with great admiration and humility that I congratulate you on twenty-five years of incredible service to the Lord and his people. The number of souls brought to the Lord through your service speaks for itself. There is no question that your leadership is providing an outstanding environment to reach out to current and future believers.

As your architect for the building program over the last seven years, I have had the pleasure of seeing your vision for a dynamic campus. The facilities you have envisioned and have already constructed are surely going to provide a safe haven, an atmosphere for fellowship, a recreational outlet, a beautiful environment and most important, a place where God's word will be taught for generations. Your campus, seen through this light, takes on a much more significant roll in God's kingdom than simply a group of buildings.

This concept became glaringly apparent to me at one of my visits during the construction of the Revel's Building. On a day that I assumed would be limited to a routine construction meeting, you invited me to say a few words to the students at your morning chapel. The theme for the day was "Spreading the Church of God". There were hundreds of students in the class and it seemed to me that the goal of most of them upon graduation was to go into the world and start a grass-roots church. In multiplying these numbers over the decades that Lancaster Baptist / West Coast Baptist College will be serving the Lord, I began to understand the importance of the "architecture" we were creating. I sincerely thank you for including me in that endeavor.

So far, the construction of the designs we have created has been delightfully executed. Again, a testament to your leadership in putting together a fantastic team. I look forward to serving with you over the next era of Lancaster Baptist / West Coast Baptist College and wish you all the best in your ministry.

Yours together in the Lord,

*Jim Bickel*

James S. Bickel, Jr. AIA

3600 BIRCH STREET . SUITE 120 . NEWPORT BEACH, CA 92660
PHONE 949. 757 - 0411          FAX 949. 757 - 0511

# South Pac Industries, Inc.

**SOUTH PAC INDUSTRIES INC.**
**44110 YUCCA AVE.**
**LANCASTER, CA 93535**

**661-951-1176**
**661-951- 9775 FAX**

Dear Pastor Chappell,

You and your wife have been a blessing to our family over the past seventeen years that we have attended Lancaster Baptist Church. You have not only been a great pastor to me over the years, but a friend who has had a great impact on my life. The leadership that you have shown has been incredible as well as the vision that you put into action with both the church and the schools. It is an honor to be part of this great church that teaches right out of the King James Bible. Your teachings enable us to take these biblical principles and make them a part of our lives. I would be remiss if I didn't mention the counsel that you have provided us over the years as it has been more solid than the Rock of Gibraltar and was always biblically sound.

Your testimony is truly remarkable and reflects the blessings that God bestows upon the faithful. It is with pride when I tell others that you are my pastor. With the pop-culture that we live in these days as well as the "gotcha" media who would love nothing better than to bring down a true man of God, I have immense gratitude for the solid foundation you bring to our church. The way in which you live your life and practice what you preach has provided us with a role model that is second to none. When naysayers from other churches say, "Look at the preacher's kids," I lovingly tell them, "Yes, look at my pastor's kids." The success you had in rearing your children gave us not only hope, but the confidence of raising them in strong Baptist values. Watching how you have prioritized your life has helped me with mine.

I am glad to see that you are changing life styles a little, so you can remain focused on the main thing, saving souls. My wife and I can happily say that all of our kids' souls are saved, and that is in large part to God being able to do his work through Lancaster Baptist Church's ministry. For that, we will forever be in your debt.

Now I can't end this without at least one reference to hunting. The times we have spent together hunting birds, and big game in Colorado was a treasure. I have to tell you, you shoot as straight as you deliver the Lord's word. I want to also thank you for allowing me to travel with you to Australia and seeing up close what our missionaries get accomplished.

Thinking of what God has done for you over the past twenty-five years, I can't even imagine what he has in store for you for the next twenty-five. Again, thanks for being my family's pastor, and a man that I can call both Pastor and Friend.

Thank you,

Dave and Anne Bradley

44111 Yucca Ave. ▪ Lancaster, CA 93535 ▪ 661 951-1176 ▪ fax 661 951-9775
▪www.southpac.com

THE **GILLEY GROUP** LLC

January 13, 2011

Pastor Paul Chappell
Lancaster Baptist Church
4020 E. Lancaster Blvd.
Lancaster, CA 93535

Dear Paul:

Congratulations on twenty five years of extraordinary service to God and our community.
It is truly a blessing to have a man such as yourself so committed to bringing the Gospel
to so many people not only in the Antelope Valley but also throughout this land. Your
direct ministry at Lancaster Baptist has drawn a huge flock but your leadership with West
Coast Baptist College has multiplied your impact into all four corners of our country.

Thank you for your steadfast, nurturing influence these past many years. We all look
forward to many more.

Sincerely,

JAMES C. GILLEY
President

44916 TENTH STREET WEST, LANCASTER CA 93534
TEL. 661.948.9612 FAX. 661.948.9613
CELL. 661.435.1114

Evangelical Christian Credit Union
955 West Imperial Highway
P.O. Box 2400
Brea, CA 92822-2400
800.634.3228    714.671.5700

w w w . e c c u . o r g

MARK G. HOLBROOK
*President / CEO*

ECCU

January 12, 2011

Pastor Paul Chappell
Lancaster Baptist Church
4020 E. Lancaster Blvd
Lancaster, CA 93535

Dear Pastor Chappell,

I rejoice with you as you celebrate twenty-five years of effective ministry at Lancaster Baptist Church. The Lord has clearly used you in countless ways to honor Him through your faithful, humble leadership these many years.

I thank God that He has allowed ECCU to play a small part in the tremendous story of Lancaster Baptist. It has been a joy and privilege to walk along side you through our banking relationship. Yet I count our personal friendship of even greater value. Your gracious encouragement and abiding friendship has meant a great deal to me over the years. Thank you.

Paul, it is a joy to join with you in acknowledging God's amazing grace and sustaining guidance so richly bestowed upon Lancaster Baptist. I am especially thankful for your godly and wise leadership. I clearly recall those very early days and look back with wonder at our Lord's faithfulness – and yours.

I pray God will grant you abundant grace as you continue to shepherd the flock of God in Lancaster in coming days and years. Again, congratulations on twenty-fives years of faithful and effective ministry.

*And when the Chief Shepherd appears, you will receive the unfading crown of glory (1 Peter 5:4).*

All for His glory,

Mark G. Holbrook
President/CEO

*Congratulations, Paul !*

Dr. Paul Chappell

Congratulations for your twenty-five years of service to the people in Lancaster area. The city has been blessed by the Lord sending you to them. Thank you for being obedient to the call of God. Many souls have been ushered into the Kingdom of God and saints strengthened in the faith. The impact of your ministry at Lancaster Baptist Church has also reached around the world.

My church Shawnee Baptist is directly blessed by the training you gave to our pastor Brother David Delaney while he served several years on your staff. You instilled in him church organization, reaching out to a lost world, training of the saints, and a compassionate love for people. Thank you, thank you!

On the personal side, it has truly been a blessing and honor to help you with building planning and construction. You have been receptive to my ideas and suggestions. I prayerfully went to every meeting with you trusting God to give you good counsel.

I pray Gods continued blessing on you, your ministry, and your family.

Your Friend,

Ron Kendall

March 15, 2011

Dear Pastor Chappell,

On behalf of all of us here at Antelope Valley Engineering, we would like to congratulate you for 25 years of service to the communities of the Antelope Valley and beyond. You have been a fine example to the people and leaders of this community. Lancaster Baptist Church and the West Coast Baptist College have experienced tremendous growth under your direction and leadership. The impact of your work is not only affecting those locally and regionally, but is also reaching out globally in epic proportions.

We have worked with you over the years to further expand the Church and various college campus facilities and have been impressed by the continual growth. We admire and truly appreciate your loyalty and faithfulness to this community and its people, but mostly for your commitment to God's service. We look forward to sharing many more memories, moments and celebrations with you as you continue to serve the Antelope Valley and the Lord's ministry.

Once again, congratulations on your 25 years of faithful service. May God continue to bless you, the Church and the College.

Sincerely,

Barry S Munz
Vice President

129 West Pondera Street • Lancaster, California 93534 • (661) 948-0805 • Fax (661) 945-8170

# POLITICAL LEADERS

**LEROY D. BACA,** SHERIFF

**County of Los Angeles**
Office of the Sheriff
4700 Ramona Boulevard
Monterey Park, California 91754-2169

January 18, 2011

Pastor Paul Chappell
Lancaster Baptist Church
4020 E. Lancaster Blvd
Lancaster, California 93535

Dear Pastor Chappell:

I would like to take this opportunity to offer my warmest congratulations on the occasion marking your 25 years of dedicated ministry. Your distinguished contribution to the community is truly commendable.

The men and women of the Los Angeles County Sheriff's Department join me in saluting your accomplishments and wishing you the very best in your future endeavors.

My kindest regards.

Sincerely,

LEROY D. BACA
SHERIFF

R. Rex Parris      Mayor
Ronald D. Smith    Vice Mayor
Sherry Marquez     Council Member
Ken Mann           Council Member
Marvin E. Crist    Council Member

Mark V. Bozigian   City Manager

March 14, 2011

Lancaster Baptist Church
4020 E. Lancaster Blvd.
Lancaster, California 93535

Dear Congregation:

*"Neither do man light a candle, and put it under a bushel, but on a candlestick; and it giveth light unto all that are in the house. Let your light so shine before men, that they may see your good works, and glorify your Father which is in Heaven,"* Matthew 5:15-16.

This verse has always been a favorite of mine since I was a child. To many in the Antelope Valley, it also describes the blessings that the Lord has provided us through Pastor Paul Chappell. For 25 years, he has tirelessly spread the Word of Jesus Christ to our community and helped thousands of people accept Jesus Christ as their savior. Unlike many others in similar positions, he has also been unafraid to declare the need to recognize and accept the Lord as a part of our everyday professions and personal lives. Lancaster and the entire Antelope Valley are so much better today because of his love for Christ and his love for his neighbors and City. It is an honor to know Pastor Chappell and to thank him for 25 years of service in giving light to all that are in the Lord's house.

Sincerely,

Mark V. Bozigian
City Manager

MVB:ad

July 1, 2011

Paul Chappell, Pastor
Lancaster Baptist Church
4020 East Lancaster Boulevard
Lancaster, California 93535

Dear Pastor Chappell:

I would like to begin this letter with my heartfelt congratulations for your truly incredible leadership during the past twenty-five years at Lancaster Baptist Church! As the Lancaster Baptist Church family celebrates a quarter century of service to the Antelope Valley, as well as to people across our nation and around the world, I hope each of you rejoice in the remarkable way God has used your congregation to impact countless lives.

While assigned as the captain at Lancaster Sheriff's Station, I witnessed first hand how your leadership helped to transform the Antelope Valley, which was striving to make itself safer and more family friendly. The community meeting you initiated at the church, attended by more than 3,000 people from all parts of the community, was the genesis for what later became the highly successful Antelope Valley Crime Fighting Initiative (AVCFI). Your continuing leadership and support, coupled with the support of your congregation, has been integral in the dramatic improvement in the quality of life throughout the cities of Lancaster, Palmdale, and the neighboring areas that make up the Antelope Valley community. These changes have drawn interest from cities and law enforcement agencies from across the country looking to achieve similar milestones in their communities.

You have been a longtime friend to all of those serving in public safety positions and their families. This has been especially true for the men and women of Lancaster Sheriff's Station. You have always been an ambassador of God's love and a constant example of the servant mentality Jesus called for in Matthew 20:26. Our station will always be in your debt for the kindness and empathy you showered on us following the tragic deaths of Deputies Steve Sorensen and Pierre Bain.

I will always be grateful to God for placing you in my life as a mentor and also having the honor of counting you as my friend! I am truly in awe as I look back and see how God has used you during the past quarter of a century. I can't wait to see what you have in store for the next twenty-five years! Please know that you and Terrie and your family are in my prayers.

Sincerely,

Carl H. Deeley, Commander (Retired)
Los Angeles County Sheriff's Department

**LIVING STONE CATHEDRAL OF WORSHIP**
**FIRST MISSIONARY BAPTIST CHURCH**
*37721 NORTH 100TH STREET EAST*
*P.O. BOX 194*
*SUN VILLAGE, CA 93543*
*(661) 944-4128   (661) 944-4857 (FAX)*
*WWW.LIVINGSTONECATHEDRAL.ORG*

SENIOR PASTOR, Bishop Henry W. Hearns
PASTORS, Thomas Carter & Jerry Miller
ELDERS, Arliss Dawson, Brian Ellsworth, AJ
Hampton, Donald Mitchell, Emmett Murrell &
Rodney Rivers
TRUSTEE BOARD CHAIRMAN, Ken Traylor
ADMINISTRATOR, Sabrina R. Scott

To the Reader of This Letter,

I met Pastor Paul Chappell many years back as he started his ministry on Lancaster Blvd, just east of Antelope Valley High School. I received many handouts by the membership of his church inviting me and countless others to know Jesus as their Lord and Savior. They did not know that I was already a believer, so I stood admiring this young man to be in full compliance with Matt 28:19-20. Later on, Pastor Paul Chappell relocated his ministry to 40th St. East and Lancaster Blvd where he was expected to meet a number of city requirements, one of which would have been an immediate expenditure of thousands and thousands of dollars.

When he came to the city, I invited him into a side room to encourage him to not be discouraged, and told him I would do whatever I could as the Vice Mayor (later the Mayor) of the city of Lancaster, to help him reach the requirements within the law. I further invited him to pray with me for the Lord to move on his behalf, and the Lord did. Pastor Chappell has invited me several times to speak to the college students and even some of the leadership of his church, and each time I was extremely honored to do so.

There is no doubt in my mind that the kingdom has been, and is being enlarged by the ministry of the Lancaster Baptist Church. Further, the city of Lancaster is being made better because of the presence of Pastor Paul Chappell and the Lancaster Baptist Church family. I am personally very proud of him and stand ready to assist him in any endeavor that he undertakes. And oh yes, he has prayed for me many times during my 18 years as Mayor and Vice Mayor of Lancaster. He has been a strong source of information to me and the church that I Pastor known as Living Stone Cathedral of Worship (100th St. East & Ave R in Sun Village Ca.)

Again I say to you Pastor Chappell, be blessed in your 25 years and just know that God is pleased and I am thankful, in Jesus name, Amen.

To God be the Glory,

Bishop Henry Hearns, Senior Pastor

---

*United in Worship  -  Committed to Service*

**COMMITTEES**
LOCAL GOVERNMENT-VICE CHAIR
ACCOUNTABILITY AND
   ADMINISTRATIVE REVIEW
JUDICIARY
NATURAL RESOURCES

# Assembly
# California Legislature

**STATE CAPITOL**
P.O. BOX 942849
SACRAMENTO, CA 94249-0036
(916) 319-2036
FAX (916) 319-2136

**DISTRICT OFFICE**
41319 12TH STREET W., SUITE 105
PALMDALE, CA 93551
(661) 267-7636
FAX (661) 267-7736

**STEVE KNIGHT**
ASSEMBLYMAN, THIRTY-SIXTH DISTRICT

VICTORVILLE CITY HALL
14343 CIVIC DRIVE
VICTORVILLE, CA 92392
(760) 843-8045
FAX (760) 843-8396

Pastor Paul Chappell                                                                 3/11/2011
Lancaster Baptist Church
25th Year Anniversary Celebration

Dear Pastor Paul Chappell:

It is my great pleasure to congratulate you on 25 years of service to our community and to your flock through Lancaster Baptist Church's Ministry.

The extraordinary accomplishments you and Lancaster Baptist have achieved are exemplified through the many resources you provide to our community, such as: your magnificent facilities for elementary through high school students; West Coast Baptist College; and, of course, the beautiful Lancaster Baptist Church itself!

In addition, you, Pastor Chappell, have worked tirelessly to improve the quality of life in the Antelope Valley through such visionary work as being a moving force behind the Antelope Valley War on Gangs, which stimulated wide public support for enhanced law-enforcement and citizen involvement to reduce crime in Lancaster and the entire Antelope Valley. None of this has gone unnoticed. The full harvest of ministries planted under your leadership were recognized by Lancaster Mayor R. Rex Parris, who designated you Lancaster's Citizen of the Year in 2009!

Now, in 2011, as you commemorate Lancaster Baptist Church's 25th Anniversary, I am joining everyone else who is proud to know you and recognize you as the centerpiece for this achievement.

Sincerely,

Assemblyman Steve Knight, 36th AD

# PALMDALE
*a place to call home*

JAMES C. LEDFORD, JR.
*Mayor*

MIKE DISPENZA
*Mayor Pro Tem*

LAURA BETTENCOURT
*Councilmember*

STEVEN D. HOFBAUER
*Councilmember*

TOM LACKEY
*Councilmember*

38300 Sierra Highway

Palmdale, CA 93550-4798

Tel: 661/267-5100

Fax: 661/267-5122

TDD: 661/267-5167

January 19, 2011

Lancaster Baptist Church
4020 E. Lancaster Blvd
Lancaster, CA 93535

To Whom it May Concern,

The purpose of this letter is to formally express my appreciation for the positive influence Pastor Paul Chappell and the Lancaster Baptist Church bring to the Antelope Valley as a community.

Besides being an advocate for Christian values, Pastor Chappell has taken an active role in speaking out against criminal conduct. Pastor Chappell has been a driving force behind organizing the good people of the Antelope Valley in an effort to combat the ravages and predatory pressures of criminal activity.

The Antelope Valley is a better place because of the example and influence of Pastor Chappell and Lancaster Baptist Church. Congratulations on your twenty-five years of blessing the lives of our Antelope Valley residents.

Sincerely,

Tom Lackey
City Council Member, City of Palmdale

*Auxiliary aids provided for*

*communication accessibility*

*pon 72 hours' notice and request.*

*w w w . c i t y o f p a l m d a l e . o r g*

# PALMDALE

*a place to call home*

James C. Ledford, Jr.
*Mayor*

Mike Dispenza
*Mayor Pro Tem*

Laura Bettencourt
*Councilmember*

Steven D. Hofbauer
*Councilmember*

Tom Lackey
*Councilmember*

38300 Sierra Highway

Palmdale, CA 93550-4798

Tel: 661/267-5100

Fax: 661/267-5122

TDD: 661/267-5167

January 19, 2011

Lancaster Baptist Church
4020 E. Lancaster Blvd
Lancaster, CA 93535

To Whom it May Concern,

Please accept my heartfelt congratulations to Lancaster Baptist Church and Pastor Paul Chappell as you celebrate your 25th anniversary.

From your humble beginnings in 1986, when your congregation consisted of a handful of families that met in the upstairs room of a building in downtown Lancaster, to today's present expansive campus location in East Lancaster where thousands attend weekly, you have built one of the largest Baptist churches in the Western United States. Furthermore, West Coast Baptist College, a ministry of your church, attracts students from across the globe.

To Pastor Chappell and the thousands of people of all ages who call Lancaster Baptist their church home, may your next 25 years be as wonderful and successful as your first 25!

Sincerely,

James C. Ledford, Jr
Mayor

*Auxiliary aids provided for*

*communication accessibility*

*pon 72 hours' notice and request.*

www.cityofpalmdale.org

R. Rex Parris — Mayor
Ronald D. Smith — Vice Mayor
Sherry Marquez — Council Member
Ken Mann — Council Member
Marvin E. Crist — Council Member

Mark V. Bozigian — City Manager

February 15, 2011


Pastor Paul Chappell
Lancaster Baptist Church
4020 East Lancaster Boulevard
Lancaster, California 93535


Dear Pastor Chappell:

It is with great pleasure I congratulate you and the Lancaster Baptist Church on the occasion of your 25th Anniversary.

Your tireless dedication, leadership and ministry of twenty-five years to the citizens of Lancaster are exemplary and have made an indelible mark on the entire Antelope Valley. My family and I have been recipients of your love, guidance and care as our pastor for over twenty years, and we thank God for you daily.

May God continue to bestow His richest blessings on you, your dear family and the Lancaster Baptist Church family for many more years to come.

*For they perceived that this work was wrought of our God. Nehemiah 6:16.*

Sincerely,

Sherry Marquez
Councilwoman

SM:ad

**R. Rex Parris** | LAW FIRM

R. Rex Parris
Robert A. Parris
Howard S. Blumenthal
Ashley N. Parris
Jason P. Fowler
Alexander R. Wheeler
Kitty K. Szeto
Douglas Han
Kaveh S. Elihu
Brendan P. Gilbert

42220 10th Street West, Suite 109 | Lancaster, CA 93534 | T: 661.949.2595 | F: 661.949.7524

February 14, 2011

Pastor Paul Chappell
Lancaster Baptist Church
4020 East Lancaster Blvd.
Lancaster CA 93535

Dear Pastor Paul:

I wanted to express my sincerest thanks and congratulate you for your twenty-five years of ministry. What an accomplishment! Words cannot express the gratitude that I have for what you have done for our community. Your hard work, selflessness and caring have turned our town into a better place, creating a great legacy that will be felt for generations to come. Your tireless efforts have made our community kinder and more supportive of all its members, regardless of creed.

You epitomize the best characteristics of faith. Thank you for setting such a fine example for us all to follow. Best wishes for many more years to come.

Sincerely,

R. Rex Parris

### SEN. GEORGE RUNNER (Ret.)
MEMBER
STATE BOARD OF EQUALIZATION
**CALIFORNIA'S TAX BOARD**

July 1, 2011

Pastor Paul Chappell
Lancaster Baptist Church
4020 East Lancaster Boulevard
Lancaster, CA 93535

Dear Pastor Chappell:

It is with the greatest pleasure that I join with you and your congregation in celebrating Lancaster Baptist Churches 25th Anniversary.

For a quarter century you have provided spiritual leadership to the Antelope Valley community, sharing the Gospel and teaching of Jesus Christ, our Savior. Through hard times and good times you have grown your congregation, helping members develop their personal relationship with Jesus Christ and serve as living examples of their faith.

The past twenty-five years have been filled with constant growth and movement, never resting or content in your level of service, Lancaster Baptist Church has continued to strive for greater diversity and strength of your ministries.

It is wonderful to join all of you in celebrating this milestone and setting our sights on further works. May God continue to bless you and Lancaster Baptist Church.

Sincerely,

SEN. GEORGE RUNNER, (Ret.)
Member, Board of Equalization

400 CAPITOL MALL, SUITE 2340, SACRAMENTO, CALIFORNIA 95814 • (916) 445-2181 • FAX (916) 327-4003
WEBSITE: www.boe.ca.gov/runner
E-MAIL: george.runner@boe.ca.gov

**California State Senate**

**SENATOR SHARON RUNNER**
SEVENTEENTH SENATE DISTRICT

SACRAMENTO OFFICE
STATE CAPITOL
SACRAMENTO, CA 95814
TEL (916) 651-4017
FAX (916) 445-4662

ANTELOPE VALLEY OFFICE
848 W. LANCASTER BLVD., SUITE 101
LANCASTER, CA 93534
TEL (661) 729-6232
FAX (661) 729-1683

VICTOR VALLEY OFFICE
14343 CIVIC DRIVE, FIRST FLOOR
VICTORVILLE, CA 92392
TEL (760) 843-8414
FAX (760) 843-8348

SANTA CLARITA OFFICE
23920 VALENCIA BLVD., SUITE 250
SANTA CLARITA, CA 91355
TEL (661) 286-1471
TEL (661) 286-1472
FAX (661) 286-2543

March 14, 2011

Pastor Paul Chappell
Lancaster Baptist Church
4020 E. Lancaster Blvd
Lancaster, CA 93535

Dear Pastor Chappell,

Congratulations on celebrating 25 years with Lancaster Baptist Church. Your church and its ministries have long been a blessing to our community.

This achievement is a testament to your strong commitment to the Lord as well as the citizens of the Antelope Valley. I am pleased to recognize you for your work and I thank you for all that you do.

I wish you the best, and I look forward to supporting your ministry for many years to come.

God bless,

**Sharon Runner**
Senator, 17th Senate District

# PROFESSIONAL
# ACQUAINTANCES

**familytalk**
*with Dr. James Dobson*

540 Elkton Drive, Suite 201
Colorado Springs, CO 80907
myfamilytalk.com

February 21, 2011

Pastor Paul Chappell
Lancaster Baptist Church
4020 East Lancaster Boulevard
Lancaster, CA 93535

Dear Pastor Chappell,

Greetings from Family Talk! I received word from Pastor Tim Christoson that Lancaster Baptist Church will be celebrating its twenty-five year anniversary this summer. Congratulations on this significant milestone! Your commitment to your congregation and community has undoubtedly impacted countless individuals.

While I am certain that you have had your share of challenges and difficulties throughout your years of service, I trust that there has been an abundance of bright and uplifting moments, as well. Regardless of what may lie ahead, I hope you will find strength and encouragement in the words of the Apostle Paul: "Therefore, my dear brothers, stand firm. Let nothing move you. Always give yourselves fully to the work of the Lord, because you know that your labor in the Lord is not in vain" (I Corinthians 15:58). May you experience many more years of joyful and fulfilling ministry!

It is an honor to be a part of this momentous occasion, Pastor Chappell. God's richest blessings to you and yours!

Sincerely,

James C. Dobson, Ph.D.
Founder and President

"By wisdom a house is built, by understanding it is established."
Proverbs 24:3

ΛWANA

February 16, 2011

Lancaster Baptist Church
4020 E Lancaster Blvd
Lancaster CA 93535

Dear LBC,

It has been a joy to know Pastor Paul for many years. In fact I had the privilege of being Paul's youth director before his family and my wife and I headed to Korea as missionaries in 1976.

I learned long ago that it is easy to take kids to live anywhere in the world simply because they have flexibility and their lives are not quite established. It is more difficult to uproot and move older youth.

However in Paul's case, he met the challenge of living internationally head on, triumphing and becoming spiritually stronger as a result. Although many young people succumb to the cultural differences and change in general, Paul became better rather than bitter.

It has been wonderful to witness all that God has done in Pastor Paul's life at Lancaster the past 25 years. I stand in awe at the goodness and greatness of our God and all that He is doing through the life of one yielded to Him.

Congratulations to all of you for a remarkable God-inspired journey together that has produced much spiritual fruit for the Kingdom of our Lord and Savior Jesus Christ. May the work continue in like fashion until He returns!

With much love and appreciation,

Jack D. Eggar
President/CEO
Awana®

JDE:da

1 East Bode Road • Streamwood, IL 60107-6658 • 630.213.2000 • www.awana.org

January 27, 2011

Pastor Paul Chappell
Lancaster Baptist Church
4020 E. Lancaster Blvd
Lancaster, Ca. 93535

Dear Pastor Paul:

What a privilege it is to have the opportunity to drop a note of congratulations to you for such a milestone in your ministry. To God be the glory! God bless you and your family as you celebrate 25 years of ministry with the wonderful people at Lancaster Baptist Church. You have led this church in such a way that God has so blessed its reputation and the work of the kingdom that you are known all over America.

We, here at First Baptist Church Woodstock and the greater Atlanta area, so appreciate your commendable work and for the way the Lord has blessed your school, your Bible conferences, and your ministry around the world.

I pray that the Lord will give you the desires of your heart that are in keeping with the will of God in these next years of service. Thank you for being faithful to the Lord Jesus, committed to His dear Word, and the work of His precious Spirit. I pray that the Lord Jesus will keep you close and clean and that He will continue to use you to make His Name more famous.

Blessings on you! Thank you for your friendship. It is always a blessing to visit with you. God bless you and your family.

Sincerely His,

Johnny Hunt
JH/rb

11905 HIGHWAY 92
WOODSTOCK, GA 30188
TEL: 770.926.4428
FAX: 770.591.2508

WWW.FBCW.ORG

# JOHN MACARTHUR

February 16, 2011

Rev. Paul Chappell
LANCASTER BAPTIST CHURCH
4020 E. Lancaster Boulevard
Lancaster, CA  93535

Dear Paul,

Congratulations on 25 years of teaching the Word of God and being a
benediction to the many who sit under your teaching and preaching!  Even as I
say that, it seems a mundane way to express a true understanding of your
ministry.  The truth is, the thanks goes to the Lord who enabled you to such
usefulness, putting you into the ministry.  The Lord has given to His beloved
church the choice gift of a noble son.

I am sure you know that, as with Paul and the Corinthians, all your people are "a
letter of Christ cared for you, written not with ink but with the Spirit of the living
God, not on tablets of stone but on tablets of human hearts" (2 Corinthians 3:3).

Long faithfulness is rare and, I'm afraid, well nigh irreplaceable.  My prayer is
that God will continue to extend your ministry until, in His plan, the last lesson
is over and it's time for your eternal reward.  Again, congratulations!

Yours for the Master,

John MacArthur
Pastor-Teacher

JM:pr

# LIBERTY
## UNIVERSITY™

School of Religion

January 25, 2011

Dr. Paul Chappell
Lancaster Baptist Church
4020 E. Lancaster Blvd.
Lancaster, CA 93535

Dear Bro. Chappell,

Congratulations on spending twenty-five years at the same church. That is miraculous considering many pastors today jump from church to church, and many churches are not satisfied to keep a pastor over a long period of time. But you have had a continuing ministry which tells me that God called you there in the first place, and second God has used you. Praise God for the continuity of your ministry.

Second, God has used you in a great way to build the church. The church has gone from a handful of a few faithful people to one of the largest Baptist congregations in the country. That is amazing, and my appreciation for you in being faithful in the ministry for the work, and also being successful. Yet, as we thank you for the great things that you have done in Lancaster, let's give all of the glory to God for it is only by His power and through His grace that we serve Him.

I trust that this twenty-fifth anniversary will be special to you and your wife. As you both look back over souls won, miracles done in the name of the Lord, as well as many victories; let's give all praise to our Lord.

But let's look to the next twenty-five years. I pray that you will be used of God to do twice as much in the next twenty-five years as you have done in the past.

May God continue to bless and use you.

Sincerely yours in Christ,

Elmer L. Towns
Co Founder and Vice President, Liberty University
Dean, Liberty Baptist Theological Seminary
Dean, School of Religion
Lynchburg, Virginia

address   1971 University Boulevard
Lynchburg, VA 24502-2269

phone   434-582-2099
fax      434-582-7459

web    www.liberty.edu/religion

### JERRY VINES
M I N I S T R I E S

February 2011

Dear Dr. Chappell,

Congratulations to you on twenty–five years as pastor of Lancaster Baptist Church. These have been years of wonderful growth and the blessings of our Lord upon your life and ministry.

I am grateful for men such as yourself who are faithful to the Word of God, love the people of God and seek to win the lost to our Saviour.

I pray the Lord will give you His richest blessings in the days ahead. The past is but prologue. May you have "fruit…much fruit…more fruit…and fruit that remains!"

In Him,
Jerry Vines

Jerry Vines Ministries
2295 Towne Lake Parkway, Suite 116 #249
Woodstock, Georgia 30189

PART 2

# 25 YEARS OF CORRESPONDENCE

*Looking Back at Encouraging Words from Faithful Friends*

# PASTORS A–I

*Greater*
## PORTLAND
### BAPTIST CHURCH
· Dr. Rick Adams, Pastor ·

Dec. 8, 1998

Dear Bro. Paul,

Just a personal note to let you know that I received your letter and yes! I am and will continue to pray for you! I still have your picture of you and your family from last year's Christmas card in my personal devotions Bible. I thank God for you and your friendship. Lord willing I will see you in Tacoma WA in Jan '99. Our theme this year is Psalm 107:23-24 and we like yourself have "Charted Our Course!" I am claiming Psm 119:165 for you and LBC! Please greet Tony and the kids for me. I love you my friend.

17800 S.E. Main Street • Portland, OR 97233
(503) 761-1136•FAX (503) 761-6971

Committed to
*Excellence*
In **MINISTRY**
II CORINTHIANS 4:7

Rick Adams

P.S. (over)

Please use this for you and the family to go out together on me. Please enjoy. Love, Rick.

**Dr . Rick Adams, Pastor**
Assistants to the Pastor
Pastor Tom Hall, Pastor Greg Adams, Pastor Brad McFeters
Pastor to the Deaf, Bob Boyd, Jr.

17800 S.E. Main Street • Portland, OR 97233 • (503) 761-1136 • FAX (503) 761-6971 • www.gpbcweb.org

March 25, 2003

Dr. Paul Chappell
Lancaster Baptist Church
4020 E Lancaster Blvd
Lancaster, CA 93535-7727

Dear Brother Chappell,

I just wanted to write and let you know how much I enjoyed being with you recently during your Wednesday night service and also your fine arts competition. I do not have words enough to express how encouraged I was to see how the good hand of our Lord is upon you and the fine ministry there at Lancaster Baptist Church.

Thank you for allowing me the privilege of preaching in your pulpit. As a pastor, I know how careful you must be and the confidence you placed in me certainly was not taken for granted. I also enjoyed being able to speak to such fine young people the following day. They not only paid good attention, but it was obvious that the Lord's presence was there.

I have been praying for you and I am sorry this letter is so late, but I have been praying that God blessed your "Streams in The Desert" Banquet in a wonderful way. I will try to give you a call in the next few days so we could chat and you can let me know how things are going.

I pray for you and the family regularly. I also wanted to say thank you to your wife for allowing me to be your guest in your home and for making Jonathan feel so welcome. There is no doubt that West Coast Baptist College is a great place to train for the ministry. I do believe Jonathan has made the decision to go there, not only with my encouragement, but the obvious sanction of the Holy Spirit.

Rest assured of my prayers to you and please greet your children and family for me. Also, thank you for the beautiful motel room and the lovely fruit basket. I was so busy while I was there, that I wasn't able to enjoy it, but my family certainly did after I arrived home.

Thank you also for the generous love offering and for taking care of my plane fare. I did not expect it, but it did meet a particular need for which I am eternally grateful. If I can ever be of any assistance to you, feel free to call anytime. Until then, I will be…

Ever Your Friend In Christ,

Dr. Rick Adams, Pastor

RTA/sbh

# GREATER PORTLAND
BAPTIST GPBC CHURCH

Home of
Greater Portland
Christian Academy

Dr. Rick Adams,
Sr. Pastor

Assistant Pastors:

Rev. Tom Hall
Dr. Greg Adams
Rev. Brad McFeters,
Rev. Bob Boyd, Jr.

17800
SE Main St.

Portland, OR
97233

Phone
503.761.1136

FAX
503.761.6971

www.gpbcweb.org

May 29, 2008

Dr. Paul Chappell
West Coast Baptist College
4010 E Lancaster Blvd
Lancaster, CA 93535-7727

Dear Dr. Chappell,

Just a note to let you know that I received your recent graduation information packet and wanted to congratulate you and your staff on the 13th Commencement Exercise for West Coast Baptist College. It hardly seems that 13 years have passed since you have started the wonderful ministry of training men and women for the ministry.

As you look back, I know you thank God for what He has done but, remember that you have pastors across America that also thank God for you and West Coast Baptist College. Keep up the good work. I pray for you and your family daily, and thank God for our friendship, as well as the Hope that our future holds, not only in God's promise, but also in His eminent return. If I can ever be of any assistance to you, feel free to call any time. Rest assured of my prayers and also be confident that I remain…

Ever Your Friend in Christ,

Dr. Richard T. Adams, Pastor

RTA/dli

Follow your heart home to GPBC!

# Thomas Road Baptist Church

Ken Adrian, Pastor

February 5, 2002

Dr. Paul Chappell
Lancaster Baptist Church
4020 East Lancaster Blvd.
Lancaster, CA 93535

Dear Paul,

I just wanted to take this opportunity to thank you for including me on your mailing list for The Baptist Voice.

I am so encouraged with what God is doing with you and your wonderful ministry in Lancaster. It is exciting to see your vision for the future of your ministry. God has used you in a great way already and I know that the future is very bright for you.

I remember when you were a student at Pacific Coast Baptist Bible College. You were certainly a promising young man then. It's exciting to see God using you in such a great way today.

You might remember my son, Tim Adrian, PC graduate in the class of 1979. He married Pam Riddle. He is pastor of Westside Baptist Church in Hutchinson, Kansas, a leading church in that city. He is averaging close to five hundred and is doing an incredible job for God.

The Lord continues to richly bless our ministry here at Thomas Road for which we are very grateful. We continue to see good and encouraging things happen. Judy and I have been here for fourteen and a half years and we are thrilled with the ministry here in Phoenix.

May God's richest blessings continue to be upon you, your family, and your ever-expanding ministry.

Sincerely,

Ken Adrian

KA/se

**"Ministering to the Entire Family"**

5735 West Thomas Road • Phoenix, Arizona 85031 • (623) 247-5735

# Lifeway Baptist Church

7821 West State Road 46 • Ellettsville, Indiana 47429
812-876-6072

Kevin Albert, *Pastor* • Tony Brown, *Music Director* • Steve Von Bokern, *Youth Pastor*

October 4, 2007

Dr. Paul Chappell
Lancaster Baptist Church
4020 E. Lancaster Boulevard
Lancaster, CA 93535

Dear Dr. Chappell,

Just a note to let you know how much I appreciate you and your commitment to the cause of Christ and our Baptist heritage. Your message at the Nationwide Fellowship was a help to me personally and I know it will make an impact nationally. As you preached I could not help but think of those men who have gone before us. I'm thankful that God has raised up men such as yourself and others to make up the hedge and stand in the gap. Keep up the great work. You are in my prayers.

Your Friend,

Kevin Albert

**GRACE BAPTIST CHURCH**

*Jeffrey Amsbaugh*
SENIOR PASTOR

*Greg Powell*
ASSOCIATE PASTOR

*Wes Carnes*
YOUTH PASTOR

*Mark Liehtke*
SPANISH PASTOR

*February 20, 2008*

**Dr. Paul Chappell**
**Lancaster Baptist Church**
**4020 E. Lancaster Blvd**
**Lancaster, CA 93535**

*Dear Dr. Chappell,*

*This is just a brief note to thank you for the opportunity to preach at Lancaster Baptist Church and for the hospitality that I was able to receive at your home after the Wednesday night service.*

*Certainly you are a mentor who has taught me a lot about the ministry. I appreciate the wonderful job that you are doing to reach Lancaster and the world. God is certainly giving you a wonderful burden for souls and a marvelous leadership ability. I appreciate the way you are using these gifts to advance the cause of our Lord.*

*If there is anything I can ever do for you I trust you will not hesitate to let me know. Once again thanks for your friendship and time we were able to spend together.*

*May God's richest blessings be yours.*

*Sincerely in Christ,*

**Jeff Amsbaugh**
**Pastor**

JA:bam

*Experience a Touch of Grace*

2915 FOURTEENTH AVENUE · COLUMBUS, GEORGIA 31904 · 706-323-1046 · FAX 706-323-8554

WWW.AMAZINGRACE.NET

**Tucson**
**BAPTIST TEMPLE**

Pastor Chappell –

I continue to pray for you and the ministries surrounding you. God has blessed in great ways over the past five months with over 50 salvation decisions and 37 baptisms. Our attendance has grown by over 100 and we now have three weekly visitation times for soulwinning and visitor follow-up. Our first-ever missions conference resulted in a $135,000 faith promise commitment. God is so good! There is much to thank the Lord.

I thank the Lord for you. Thank you for being such an example! I have <u>greatly</u> missed seeing you and having personal interaction. I am planning a trip next

Brent D Armstrong, Pastor
www.mytbt.cc | www.brentdarmstrong.com

➝

spring to bring students to visit WCBC. My daughter will be a student next fall. She is already working on her paperwork. Jonathan, my youngest, cannot wait until he can come and train to be a youth pastor.

Thank you again –

Brent

"I will mention the lovingkindness of the Lord, and the praises of the Lord, according to all that the Lord hath bestowed on us"
Isaiah 62:7

145

**BAPTIST CHURCH**

Loving God. Loving Others. Labouring Together.

July 7, 2010

Dear Bro. Chappell,

My wife and I recently celebrated the 25th anniversary of our salvation (May 9, and June 1, 1985). This time has gone by so quickly and so much has happened! It was Bro. Turner who led Terrie to Christ, and got me to realize my lost condition so that later that evening I prayed with my wife asking the Lord to save me.

Over the years I have learned just how important that time right after salvation is to new believers – you know, baptism and discipleship. I will never forget all the occasions that you and Bro. Turner came to our home to visit and encourage us to grow in grace. I couldn't tell you what we talked about when you came by, but I remember that it served as an encouragement for us to get in church! I remember being impressed that you were willing to drive the 20+ miles to come to our home.

Those early years of memories and mentoring and fellowship help tie us in the church, and I want you to know that God worked through you to help us get established. I was recently sharing with some of the men in our church of the frailty of some of the new converts that missed our Bible study, only to reflect on my early days remembering how "two men" in particular didn't give up on me and my family. Only God knows the full impact and what a tremendous influence you've had on you've had on my life continue to have over these past 25 years.

My wife and I are eternally grateful for your investment in our lives, and in the lives of our children and grandchildren especially now as they have served under your ministry! Thank you and may the Lord richly bless you.

We love you – your friends,

David and Terrie Azzarello

PO Box 246, Oakdale, CA 95361
209-845-9688 | lbcoakdale@gmail.com | www.lbcoakdale.com
David Azzarello, Pastor

5811 Hoffmans Lane • Bailey's Crossroads, Virginia 22041 • (PH) 703.845.0017 • (FAX) 703.845.0020 • www.coeba.org

## Crossroads
Baptist Church

April 13, 2009

Dr. Paul Chappell
Lancaster Baptist Church
E. Lancaster Blvd.
Lancaster, CA 93535

Dear Brother Chappell,

I want to thank you for the wonderful hospitality shown Kenny, TJ, Peter and me by you and your staff during our stay in Lancaster for your recent youth conference. It was a joy for me to once again witness how the Lord is using you at Lancaster Baptist Church and West Coast Baptist Church.

The facilities are beautiful and there is such clear evidence of your leadership seen in those who are on your ministerial staff as well as those who simply serve in any capacity. Lancaster Baptist Church and West Coast Baptist College certainly provide a modern day landmark of Biblical Christianity that is to be admired.

I want to personally thank you for taking time out of your busy schedule to fellowship with me. I enjoyed the time at your beautiful home. Terri did a fine job putting everything together and she certainly has the gift of hospitality.

Thank you for the hotel room, meals and special round of golf with Dr. Sisk. I have never played on a course where I had a caddy. What a special treat! Your kindness and generosity will always be remembered.

Peter and TJ are looking forward to being at West Coast this fall. They are very special to us and we feel very comfortable with the training they will receive there. We are raising up a generation of young people that I believe will help change our world. It is good to know that there are places that can help us train them for what the Lord has for them to do.

Thank you for your friendship. I look forward to other times together in the future.

Because of Christ,

Dr. Louis C. Baldwin

Home of:

**COEBA**
& Crossroads Christian Schools

# People's
## Baptist Church

1621 Greenville Blvd. SW • Greenville, NC 27834
252.756.2822

July 17, 2008

Dr. Paul Chappell
Lancaster Baptist Church
4020 E. Lancaster Blvd.
Lancaster, CA 93535

Dear Brother Chappell,

I pray that you are doing well and that God continues to bless you and your ministry. I prayed much for you this week as you were in the midst of your leadership conference. I know all went well. I sure wish that I could have been there but was unable to come this year.

I wanted to write you to thank you for the great book you had mailed to me. I have already begun to read through the book, "The Spiritual Leader!" I know that it will prove to be a great help and blessing to me. And, I am sure that it will have a wide range of influence across America and around the world. I pray that God would use it in a wonderful way.

I praise the Lord for all the God has been able to accomplish through you. I pray for you regularly and hold you in the highest esteem. Your friendship has meant so much to me during the years and I personally thank you for all your kindness to me.

I look forward to seeing you at the Sword Conference and again at the Nationwide Independent Baptist Fellowship meeting in October. Please pray that God would honor our efforts for the fellowship meeting this fall.

Thanks again for the book! You are a very considerate and kind person!

Sincerely,

Max Barton

Max Barton

Dr. Max Barton, Pastor

## Real People . . . Real Passion

# Tabernacle Baptist Church
## Ministries

**717 NORTH WHITEHURST LANDING ROAD
VIRGINIA BEACH, VIRGINIA 23464**
*TELEPHONE: (804) 420-5476*

July 13, 1988

**ROD BELL**
*Founder & Pastor*

**PASTORAL STAFF**

**CARL D. BIEBER**
*Administrator*
Tabernacle Baptist Schools

**EDWARD G. CAUGHILL**
*Academic Dean*
Tabernacle Baptist Bible Institute

**GORDON R. COOK**
*Youth Director*
Tabernacle Baptist Church

**JOHN S. JENNINGS**
*Visitation Pastor '&*
 *Director of Evangelism*
Tabernacle Baptist Church

Rev. Paul Chappell
Lancaster Baptist Church
304 West Lancaster Blvd.
Lancaster, CA 93534

Dear Brother Chappell:

Thank you for your letter.  I apologize for being
so late in sending the requested information.  We
have had a change in secretaries and this is the
reason for the delay.  I am enclosing the address
to where you can get the Spurgeon books.

Concerning the T.E.A.M. Program – I have just been
able to really get into it and looking it over.
I would like to say that I think it is one of the
most effective, scriptural tools or methods that
I have ever seen to get every member involved in
the great commission, witnessing and soul winning.

I want to urge you to try to get it into every preacher's
hands that you possibly can.  I think it will be
greatly blessed of the Lord.

Once again, please let me apologize for the delay.
I am so sorry that I have not followed through with
what I promised.  I am praying for you and your ministry
daily.  God's hand is upon you.  Stay faithful and
He will use you.

Your friend,

Rod Bell
Pastor

RLB/lb
Enclosure

NEW CHURCH PLANTING ● MISSIONS ● PUBLICATIONS ● CASSETTE TAPES ● BOOK STORE
BIBLE INSTITUTE ● CHRISTIAN SCHOOL (K-5 - 12) ● PRESCHOOL ● MILITARY MINISTRY

# Brook Hollow Baptist Church

Russell Jones, Pastor                                    Dr. Clyde H. Box, Pastor Emeritus

Dr. Paul Chappell
Lancaster, CA.

Dear Brother Paul:

I had a wonderful time being with you
and preaching in your great church. I
do not know when I have enjoyed myself
more. Thank you for the fruit basket,
the nice room, the food, the sweet fellowship,
and the great Love offering. I enjoyed having
dinner with your precious family...I have never
felt more "at home" in my Life. I know that
you are greatful to God for the family He
has given you.

Brother Paul, I can see the hand of God upon
you and your ministry. I believe that God has
something very special for you in the future.
I love you and your family very much and
I pray for you daily.

His & Yours,

Clyde

135 West Wintergreen Road, DeSoto, Texas 75115 • (214) 298-4646

**FAIRFAX BAPTIST** *Temple*

6401 Missionary Lane
Fairfax Station, VA 22039-1859

tel. 703.323.8100
fax. 703.250.8600

FBTMinistries.org

Troy R. Calvert, Pastor
Dr. Bud Calvert, Founder

April 7, 2008

Dr. Paul Chappell
Lancaster Baptist Church
4010 E. Lancaster Blvd.
Lancaster, CA 93535

Dear Bro. Chappell,

It was great to see you again last week at the Church Planting Conference. I really appreciate your having such a great meeting in your college. It shows your heart for World Evangelism, for which I am grateful.

My special thanks to you and your wife for inviting me over to your lovely home. As always, it was a wonderful time of fellowship and a great time of personal enjoyment as well (eating!). Thanks also for the goody basket in the room and the beautiful Bible. I know I will enjoy it! Again, you and your people are gracious hosts!

I'm sorry I wasn't able to join all of you for golf on Friday morning. Without a doubt that was the greatest temptation that I have endured this year! More than the golf, though, I am sorry I missed a good opportunity to fellowship with you again. Did you tell me that you usually play some after the Leadership Conference? If so, could I join you?

Thanks again for giving me the opportunity to preach to your people. God is doing a great work through you, for which I praise the Lord.

May God continue to keep His hand upon you.

In His Name,

*Bud Calvert*
TH

Bud Calvert,
A Servant of God

BC:th

*Personally dictated, but signed in the Pastor's absence.*

Baptist Church

January 28, 1999

Lancaster Baptist Church
Pastor Paul Chappell
4020 E. Lancaster Blvd.
Lancaster, CA 93535

Dear Paul:

I just wanted to thank you again for all that you did to make my ordination service a special one. I appreciated your message. It is my desire to accomplish everything you mentioned. Please express to your deacons my gratitude for their part in the evening.

I wanted to send this check to help with the dormitory project. West Coast Baptist College is a exciting place and I look forward to recommending it to those within our church that God calls to ministry.

I believe in what you are doing and trying to do. I love you and thank God for you. If there is ever anything I can do to be a help or blessing just let me know.

Your Brother:

Steve

**Come Grow With Us...**

300 Carlsbad Village Dr. Ste. 108A PMB 154 • Carlsbad, CA 92008
(760) 754-2302 • coastline@pobox.com • Steve Chappell, Pastor

# Pastor Steve Chappell

July 18, 2006

Dear Paul,

I just wanted to thank you for hosting the Leadership Conference once again. Each year I leave with so many new ideas and an encouraged heart. I truly believe this year's conference was the best yet. Each message spoke to my heart, and the highlight of the preaching was your message on Monday evening. I was also grateful for the opportunity to teach a session on Thursday morning.

Thank you for letting me travel with you to Mark's funeral service. I know that he will be sorely missed, but you handled the service in a powerful way. I know that Mark was pleased with the events of that day and the many souls that were saved. I pray for you everyday.

Your brother,

Steve

Coastline Baptist Church ~ 557 Vista Bella
Oceanside, CA 92057
(760) 754-2302 ~ coastlinebaptist.com

806-798-2723 **Dr. H. Frank Collins** 4001 88th Place
Lubbock, TX 79423

April 30, 001

Dr. Paul Chappel
Lancaster Baptist Church
4020 Lancaster Blvd.
Lancaster, Ca. 93535

Dear Friend Paul,

You could never imagine what a delight it was for me to receive
your letter. Yes, I remember the hamburger and the shoes. If
I could have been where you are I would have done it again this
year. I had a delightful day with Randy Alonso  who pastors
near me. We played the country club golf course and it was such
a beautiful day. He was on my staff at Calvary.

I am sure that you have found out and will find out more in
the future the spirit of ungratefulness that exists in the
ministry today. Young men that I really led the church to
sacrifice for pass right through town or perhaps minister at
a local church and never call. One must just keep on sowing.
Some of the seed will produce rich harvests.

On July 15th I will go back to Calvary (first time back) for
the ordination of a young man that grew up under my ministry.
When I retired I asked the Lord to give me one more preacher
and one more missionary. That prayer has been 50% answered with
Kenny's ordination. Now for the missionary!

I hear such wonderful things about your ministry. I must say
that I expected it from you.

The next time we can be together lunch and another pair of shoes
are on me. How beautiful are the feet of those who preach the
gospel. At least I can put a pair of shoes on them.

Your friend,

H. Frank Collins

*Pastor Emeritus*
*Calvary Baptist Church*

# *I*ndependent
# *B*aptist
# *C*hurch

9255 Piscataway Road ❑ P.O. Box 206 ❑ Clinton, Maryland 20735

**T. Michael Creed**
Pastor

**301-856-1616**
Phone

**301-856-8234**
Fax

**www.IBCMINISTRIES.org**
Internet

**IBC@IBCMINISTRIES.org**
E-mail

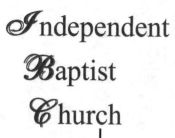

December 7, 2004

Dr. Paul Chappell
Lancaster Baptist Church
4020 E. Lancaster Blvd.
Lancaster, CA 93535

Dear Bro. Chappell,

I just wanted to thank you and your staff for the wonderful time that my wife and I had at the pastor's retreat. It was definitely a sharpening time in my life; and a great opportunity to see my son and to see the spiritual steps that he has taken in his life. I am asking God to use him greatly in the future.

Thank you again for the meals, the materials, and the leadership helps that we received. It will probably take me the rest of this year to follow up on the books and the reading material and go through the things that were given to us; but I know that it will be a great help in the ministry as we move forward for the Lord here in Clinton, Maryland. We appreciate your friendship!

Sincerely,

Pastor T. Michael Creed

TMC:sg

*A*nd he said unto them, Go ye into all the world, and preach the gospel to every creature.
*M*ark 16:15

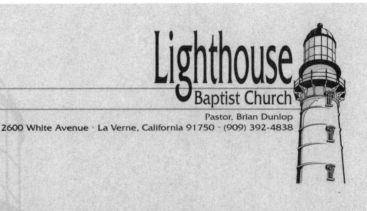

**Lighthouse**
Baptist Church
Pastor, Brian Dunlop
2600 White Avenue · La Verne, California 91750 · (909) 392-4838

DEAR PASTOR CHAPPELL,

I RECEIVED THE COPY OF "GUIDED BY GRACE"
THAT YOU MAILED TO ME. I TOOK IT HOME WITH
ME LAST NIGHT AND READ SOME CHAPTERS.
THANK YOU FOR SENDING IT. WHAT I HAVE READ
THUS FAR HAS BEEN A BLESSING. IT IS A NEEDED
MESSAGE FOR OUR AGE. THANK YOU ALSO FOR THE
LOVE OFFERING. IT WAS BOTH GENEROUS AND A
BLESSING FOR MY FAMILY AND ME. THANK YOU
FOR YOUR KINDNESS. MAY GOD BLESS YOU AS YOU
SERVE HIM.

IN CHRIST,

Brian Dunlop

*II Corinthians 4:6 "For God. . . commanded the light to shine out of darkness"*

# HERITAGE

## BAPTIST CHURCH

*Home of Heritage Christian School*

14510 Spriggs Road • Woodbridge, Virginia 22193 • Phone: (703) 680-6629
Fax: (703) 670-4369 • http://hbchcs.org

January 19, 2007

Dr. Paul Chappell
Lancaster Baptist Church
4020 East Lancaster Blvd.
Lancaster, CA 93535

Dear Brother Chappell,

I trust this letter finds you and your family doing well. We pray for you and the ministry regularly and are thankful for the privilege of being able to send some of our young people to West Coast Baptist College.

Please do not feel it necessary to respond to this letter; I simply want to thank you and hopefully be a small encouragement. I have just finished reading, "Grace For Godly Living", and want you to know that I thought it was outstanding. There really is a wonderful place of grace that lies between legalism and license; and Brother Chappell, you have done a great job in putting it into words. It took me too many years to really understand that place and I hope this book shortens the journey for young preachers. We are going to incorporate the book into the Pastoral Theology reading list in our Institute.

What you do matters more than you know. Keep doing it.

In Christ,

Pastor Michael E. Edwards

*"Thy testimonies have I taken as an __Heritage__ forever:*
*for they are the rejoicing of my heart."*
*Psalm 119:111*

# Grace
## BAPTIST CHURCH

July 26, 2010

Dr. Paul Chappell
Lancaster Baptist Church
4020 Lancaster Blvd.
Lancaster, CA 93535

Dear Dr. Chappell,

Thank you for coming to Grace Baptist for our 50th Anniversary Sunday. Your messages were right on target. Our people were refreshed and went out saying, "it was good to be in the house of the Lord." The day was a huge success and we appreciate you, your wife and Matt for being a part of it.

We appreciate also the wonderful testimonies we hear about the college. Our students come home excited to see family, but ready to come back to school with high hopes of what the Lord will do in their lives while at school.

May God continue to bless in your life, your family's lives and the college.

Warmest regards,

Dr. Bill Egerdahl
Pastor

*Brother Chappell,*
*What a blessing to have you! You*
*and your family + church (+ school) are*
*continually in our prayers. May Gods*
*power + protection be upon you*
*Bill & Vicki*

416 Denham Avenue | West Columbia, SC 29169 | 803.794.8237 | www.gbcwc.org

**THAT GOD MAY BE ALL IN ALL**

## Pacific Baptist Church

December 17, 1999

**Joe Esposito,**
**Pastor**

2474 Pacific Ave.
Long Beach
California 90806

**Home of**
**Pacific Christian**
**School**

Cambodian Ministry

Spanish Ministry

Teen Ministry

Children Ministry

Singles Ministry

(562) 424-7714

Fax: (562) 424-3324

Pastor Paul Chappell
4020 E. Lancaster Blvd.
Lancaster, CA 93535

Dear Brother Chappell,

I just wanted to thank you again for faithfully serving the Lord and being an example to many pastors here on the West Coast and around the country. Thank you for your willingness to help other pastors. You have been an encouragement to me personally and your ministry there has been an unbelievable help in every area that I can possible think of from our youth to our singles to our couples…music, spirit of excellence, aggressive soul winning, follow up, discipleship, etc. If there is ever anything I can do for you, please let me know.

Sincerely,

*Joe Esposito*

Pastor Joe Esposito
JE/me

*"The righteous shall flourish like the palm tree:"  Psalm 92:12*

# LIGHTHOUSE

### Baptist Church

October 2, 2000

Dr. Paul Chappell
Lancaster Baptist Church
4020 Lancaster Blvd.
Lancaster, CA 93535

Thank you for keeping Lighthouse Baptist Church and me in your prayers. Only heaven will tell how much you have been a help to me personally and to LBC corporately. My staff, volunteer leaders, and I have been coming to training sessions at your church for years. I believe much of the success the Lord has granted us here at Lighthouse is due to what we have learned from you.

We just completed our annual bus days promotion. Each year we dedicate four to six weeks of emphasis on our bus ministry and reaching all that we can through our buses. This year we were blessed to have 1,427 ride our buses on September 24th with 101 saved. There were a total of 2,233 in attendance that day. During the 4 week push there were @185 people saved in the bus church services alone. Our Spanish department also saw @70 saved during this time.

I say all of this to let you see a small portion of how much your prayers and commitment to helping other churches has impacted Lighthouse Baptist Church. Please continue to pray for us as we shift gears and prepare for our November 19th Big Day. Dr. Dave Gibbs will be our guest speaker and we are looking forward to a rich harvest of souls on that day as well. We will again blow the trumpet and gather the whole church to go after the drive-in crowd.

Brother, I am eternally grateful for your friendship and mentoring. Like you, I want my life to count for the glory of God and I want to help the people God has gathered at LBC to have the best Judgement Seat of Christ possible. Thank you for the part you have played in this endeavor.

Your Friend in the Ministry,

Doug Fisher
Pastor

DAF/jfw

1345 Skyline Drive, Lemon Grove, CA 91945 ●(619) 461-5561
http://www.lighthousebaptist.com ● Doug Fisher, Pastor

# CLEVELAND
## BAPTIST CHURCH

### PREACHING CHRIST • REACHING THE WORLD

July 22, 2010

Dr. Paul Chappell
Lancaster Baptist Church
4020 E. Lancaster Boulevard
Lancaster, California 93535

Dear Bro. Chappell,

I want to begin by thanking you, the staff, and the Lancaster Baptist Church family for hosting one of the greatest meetings I have ever attended. This year's Leadership Conference was outstanding. Each moment on campus was a tremendous blessing and was used of the Lord to encourage me. Denise and I left physically tired but spiritually refreshed. I am sure you and the staff had to be encouraged by the numbers and spirit of the meeting.

One thing that makes this conference so special is that it seems to draw a broad spectrum of people from every camp and school in our independent Baptist world. I love that fact and the fellowship it brings with like-minded men; each year I meet new people. I love the openings each night with the powerful music, drama, video, and congregational singing, but most of all, I love the preaching which stirs a great desire in me to serve the Lord. Thank you for the work and expense it takes to make this conference a reality.

I would also like to thank you for giving me the opportunity to speak at one of the sessions. It was a real honor to stand before other men in the ministry and encourage them to uplift other preachers in the ministry.

Denise and I are so thankful for the wonderful room at the Hampton Inn, the nice basket, and gifts. We also enjoyed the meals and the host of other things you did to show grace and hospitality. Thank you for the honorarium for speaking, the $50.00 gift card to Olive Garden given to each senior pastor, and the rose that was given to each preacher's wife; these things were generous and kind.

I will be praying for next year's 25th anniversary conference, and I am excited about attending. Denise and I will also be praying about going on the Alaskan cruise next year. It should be a lot of fun and a marvelous opportunity to be with God's people.

Thank you again for being my friend and for encouraging so many others across the face of this world to love and serve the Lord in greater ways. Denise and I love you, Terrie, and your family. We love what God is doing there. Hope you have a marvelous summer, and I look forward to hosting you in September.

Your friend,

Kevin Folger
Pastor

4431 Tiedeman Rd. Brooklyn, Ohio 44144 • (216) 671-2822 • www.clevelandbaptist.org • Kevin Folger, Pastor

# HERITAGE
## BAPTIST CHURCH

2960 Merced Street, San Leandro, CA 94577

March 11, 2005

Dr. Paul Chappell
Lancaster Baptist Church
4020 E. Lancaster Blvd.
Lancaster, CA 93535

Dear Dr. Chappell,

Words cannot describe the depths of my gratitude to you for preaching my ordination service this past Tuesday evening. Your guidance and involvement led to a night that glorified our Lord in a wonderful way. Everything flowed very smoothly: there was the evidence of the power of God on all aspects of what occurred that night.

When I look back in retrospect of the Lord's working in my life these past few years, invariably much of the major accomplishments point to the profound influence you have personally had in my life. Thank you for the investment of time and counsel that you have placed in me. Most especially, thank you for being a loving friend to me.

I am looking forward to what the Lord will see fit to work through Grace and I in the years ahead. Each week I have been privileged to see some new aspect of His power and grace flow through this ministry. I do not take lightly the awesomeness of the responsibility placed on me for reaching the unsaved masses of people around us, and in being a loving and faithful undershepherd.

Please express my thankfulness to the Lancaster Baptist Church family and your wonderful staff for their loving expressions of encouragement and prayers. Please also accept my thankfulness for the floral gift from you and Mrs. Chappell.

As always, you, your family, and the church are in my prayers continually. I will be forwarding to you separate from this letter a love gift from Grace and I towards the building expansion offering that is being taken.

Again, thank you for everything. I look forward to seeing you before the Spiritual Leadership Conference, and to speaking with you again soon.

Your Friend,

Alan D. Fong
Pastor

Office  510 357-7023

Email  info@hbc.org

A Place to Belong...A Place to Grow...A Place to Be Loved...

# Barstow Baptist Temple

511 Victor Ave, Barstow, CA 92311 (760)-252-4692 Fax: (760)-252-7873 email: bbtal@juno.com

July 21, 2004

Dr. Paul Chappell
Lancaster Baptist Church
4020 E. Lancaster Blvd.
Lancaster, CA 93535

Dear Bro. Chappell,

I want to say thank you for the Spiritual Leadership Conference. It was a tremendous conference, and Monday night was an emotional time for all that was there. I spent twenty years in the Marine Corps, and during that time saw many young men give their lives fighting for the freedom of people. The spiritual impact on those from my church, and myself that attended was great.

Bro. Chappell thank your people for all their hard work in making the conference a success. I know that you and your people spent many hours seeing that every thing was taken care of, and went smoothly. When you awarded the Compassion Award I thought of your people, and if there was an Unselfish Award it should go to them.

Thank you for your friendship. My life and ministry has been blessed from knowing you. Thank you for your firm stand, and for building a **great church.** May God continue to richly bless you, your family, and ministries.

Your Friend,

A.D. Hampton
Pastor

| A.D. Hampton | Norm Markley | Dino Silva | Jeff Climer | Barney Williams |
|---|---|---|---|---|
| Pastor | School Administrator | Spanish Minister | Bus Ministry | Youth Director |

# Barstow Baptist Temple

511 Victor Ave., Barstow, CA 92311  (760)-252-4092  Fax: (760)-252-7873  email: info@barstowbaptist.com

August 25, 2010

Dr. Paul Chappell
Lancaster Baptist Church
4020 E. Lancaster Blvd.
Lancaster, CA 93535

Drear Bro. Chappell,

What a tremendous blessing that you would send your mechanic and helper to repair one of our buses.  I want to tell you from the bottom of my heart how much your help is appreciated.  Bro. Chappell your love for people, and for the ministry of the Barstow Baptist Temple is a blessing not only to me but so many others.  The bus that was repaired brings in from 40 to 60 people each Sunday.  Having a bus ministry yourself you understand what it means to those that depend on our buses in order to come to church.  To say thank you seems so inadequate, so I want to say that not every one has a friend like you.

Bro. Chappell your friendship is something that I will always cherish.  May God bless you, Your family and your ministry.

Your Friend,

A.D. Hampton
Pastor

ADH/sh

| A. D. Hampton | Haion Lundy | Dino Silva | Jeff Cliner |
|---|---|---|---|
| Pastor | Assistant Pastor | Spanish Minister | Bus Director |

# Hardy

July 28, 2009, 2009

Dear Bro. Chappell,

I wanted to take this opportunity to thank you for the opportunity to address the Masters Class and to speak during chapel earlier this year. Both were an honor and a delight. I am aware that there is no shortage of men who would be glad to speak at West Coast.

Let me also thank you for giving yourself to a great cause. I continue to be amazed at all the good things that have happened at Lancaster during your tenure. Simultaneously, I am amazed at all the bad things happening in our country and culture. It seems like it was only yesterday that I sat in a class on prophecy at BBC questioning why the most powerful nation on earth couldn't be indentified in the end times. The possibility that America would no longer be a major player was broached, but I must confess, deep inside, I dismissed that thought. I just couldn't conceive of such a thing. Now it seems more like a probability than a possibility.

Bro. Chappell, none of us know what the next few years hold for us. It may be that our real mettle will be tested. With that thought in mind, there are two things that cheer and encourage my heart. First and foremost is the sovereignty of God as it relates to the future and the only real product of the universe - the people of God. I know His purposes for us will not be frustrated. Second, God has blessed me beyond measure with friendships. That is, He has allowed me to rub shoulders with the best people on earth. You have been very gracious to me Bro. Chappell and I want you to know that I have been praying for you virtually every day for three years or so. I am sure your workload is great and I ask God for strength for you. But even more, I ask God to make you immovable in godliness/holiness and I ask Him to give you a special friend or friends you can bare your heart with. The more a man grows, in whatever area, the lonelier it can become.

Also, two pastors I have encouraged your way have attended the Leadership Conference and one (Bruce Humbert) has scheduled you to speak I believe. I am working on more and think they will eventually attend. In closing, I wish you God's very best. If there is ever anything I can do for you I trust you will not hesitate to ask.

Yours In Christ,

Dave Hardy

Hardy Ministries • P.O. Box 36, Stillwater, OK 74076 • www.hardyministries.com
918-232-1864 • 918-809-5519 • 405-372-7444 • dhardy@stillwaterbbc.org

165

## BIBLE BAPTIST CHURCH

October 17, 2009

**Wayne Hardy**
Pastor

**Jason Jett**
Music & Youth
Director

**Ryan Rench**
Missions Intern

**Austin Pollard**
Missions Intern

**Jeremy Reagan**
Missions Intern

**April Collier**
Pastor's Secretary

**Jamie Rench**
Church Secretary

Pastor Paul Chappell
Lancaster Baptist Church
4020 E Lancaster Blvd.
Lancaster, CA  93535

Bro. Chappell,

I want to thank you for the wonderful opportunity to preach at West Coast Baptist College and Lancaster Baptist Church the last couple of days. Both were an honor and sincere privilege. The folks were great to preach to and very receptive. I expected nothing different. I hope the messages were able to be a help and encouragement to them. As I told them, it is a little daunting to preach the Wednesday night after you had over 5,000 in church and 700-800 visitors. Since I preached the Book, I can only assume they needed it somehow. I hope it will encourage them for the remaining Sundays in the month. I admit it made it a little easier since you preached on the Great Whore of Revelation 17 on a big Sunday morning. Nothing I preached would be thought unusual after that!

Thank you, as well, for the famous hospitality of Lancaster. The basket was the greatest because it had books in it. Anything with books is a wonderful gift. Thank you for the unexpected Bible. My old Scofield is falling apart and that one will serve as a great replacement. The meals with the staff were a great encouragement. It is undoubtably true that men go further when they gather good men around them. You have some of the best. I appreciate the time with them.

I trust you enjoyed your time in Oklahoma. I hope you left it in better shape than you found it. There are more similarities to California all the time!

One of the closing points I made to the church dealt with the Pyramid Principle. The pyramid is so strong because in order to build it higher, you have to build it wider at the base. I tried to encourage the folks to realize that you had enough vision to go a long way, but they need to be constantly widening the base so that Lancaster can continue to rise high in Fundamentalism and be a strong voice and example. I trust that will continue to be true.

Thank you for the love offering and the opportunity to preach. I trust that Lancaster's best days are ahead. Keep up the good work.

For His glory,

Wayne Hardy

E. Virginia & N. Jardot  |  P.O. Box 1985  |  Stillwater, OK 74076
Phone 405.372.7444  |  Fax 405.377.7948  |  info@stillwaterbbc.org

**TRI-CITY**
MINISTRIES

BAPTIST CHURCH

CHRISTIAN
SCHOOLS

WORLD-WIDE
MISSIONS

PASTOR:
CARL D. HERBSTER

June 1, 2006

Pastor Paul Chappell
Lancaster Baptist Church
4020 Lancaster Blvd.
Lancaster, CA 93535

Dear Brother Paul:

I am just recently back from a trip to Romania where I had the privilege of presenting the first diplomas to the graduates of the Independent Baptist College of Romania. While I was there I had the opportunity to spend some time with Tim Tyler and his family. I know they are missionaries sent out by your church. I wanted to write and let you know what a great job they are doing in the college and in their efforts to plant an Independent Baptist Church in Timisoara, Romania. I am very thankful for their commitment to the Lord, to their family, and to the work of Jesus Christ in Romania. I wanted to let you know what an outstanding job your missionaries are doing reaching Romania for Jesus Christ. Thank you for your commitment to reach your community and the world with the Gospel.

I also want to commend you for the good work you are doing in training young people here in the United States. My sons and I have had the opportunity to come in contact with several West Coast graduates and present students. We are pleased with the commitment we see in these young people. I know it is not easy running a Christian college as well as pastoring a vibrant church. However, God is using you in a wonderful way and I am very thankful to call you my friend. We pray for you often and trust the Lord will continue to bless you, your family, and your ministry.

I still hope to bring my staff to Lancaster sometime in the future to learn more about your outreach program. I want our church to be on fire for evangelism. I believe there is much we could learn from you and your people. I hope to contact you soon to work out some dates for me and my staff to visit your ministry.

Thanks again for your commitment to the Lord Jesus Christ and His work. May God continue to bless you and use you.

Your friend and co-laborer,

Carl D. Herbster

CDH/gh

PS: I am enclosing one of the most recent CD's my sons produced. As you notice by the back cover, I am singing with them on a few songs. Miracles never cease!

"A CHURCH
WITH A HEART,
IN THE HEART
OF AMERICA."

*www.tri-city.org*

4500 LITTLE BLUE PARKWAY    INDEPENDENCE, MO 64057    816-795-8700

# PASTORS J–R

# First Baptist Church

14400 Diamond Path West
ROSEMOUNT, MINNESOTA 55068-0089
Phone 651/423-2271  Fax 651/423-4471
Email: FBCRSMT@aol.com
www.FBCRSMT.org

MINISTRIES:

*Christian School*

*Bus*

*Sunday School*

*Youth*

*Music*

*Children's Church*

*Nursing Home*

*Missionary*

*Soulwinning*

*Summer Camp*

*Jail*

*Master Club*

*Deaf*

*Spanish*

October 20, 2006

Dr. Paul Chappell
President
West Coast Baptist College
4010 E. Lancaster Blvd.
Lancaster, CA 93535

Dear Brother Chappell:

Just a personal note to thank you for the privilege it was to spend a few days at West Coast Baptist College and Lancaster Baptist Church.

Everytime I am here my heart rejoices to see how God is continuing to bless and use you for His glory. It was a delight to be in the last service of your Missionary Conference and to hear Brother Sisk preach that powerful message. I know you rejoice that he is there with you influencing the lives of our next generation of laborers, as Jesus tarries His coming.

Thank you so much for the honorarium you gave me and for taking care of my travel expenses. The motel room was very comfortable as well as "quiet" which I greatly appreciated.

Let me also thank you for your special hospitality on Wednesday night after that wonderful service. Ellie and I greatly enjoyed the fellowship and food. I want you to know it meant much to both of us for you to also invite the young people from First Baptist Church.

God bless you as you continue to faithfully serve Him. I want you to know that we shall be praying for you and your ministry in the days ahead. Please don't hesitate to call upon me if I can be of any help to you in any way.

With best wishes and personal kindest regards I remain:

Sincerely your friend & co-laborer,

Ed Johnson, Jr.
Pastor Emeritus

EJ:pjd

*"Every Visitor an Honored Guest"*

169

# North Love Baptist Church

**5301 E. Riverside Boulevard**
*Rockford, IL 61114*
*(815) 877-6021*

PAUL KINGSBURY
Senior Pastor
DANIEL R. OUTLER
Assistant Pastor
JIM WHITTENBURG
Youth Pastor
TOM SEELEY
School Administrator

July 18, 2003

**Dr. Paul Chappell, Senior Pastor**
**Lancaster Baptist Church**
*4020 E. Lancaster Boulevard*
*Lancaster, California 93535*

**Dear Dr. Chappell,**

*Thank you for a great conference! Everything was superb! I bought a complete set of the event and have already begun distributing the information to our staff.*

*I pray for you regularly and appreciate your balanced approach to life and ministry. Thanks again for the invitation to Palm Springs following the conference. I trust you folks had a great time. I hope you will ask again.*

*We are looking forward to you speaking here on* **November 5, 2003***, in behalf of Reformers Unanimous and Envision The Vision 2003.*

*Next July we hope to bring many other staff personnel to the Leadership Conference. God bless and keep you in His care.*

**Your friend and fellow servant,**

**Paul Kingsbury**

*ll*

**"...to seek and to save that which was lost"**

# PEOPLES • BAPTIST • CHURCH

**Dr. David A. McCoy,** PASTOR

850 Mill Road, McDonough, GA 30253
Telephone (770) 914-7388/Fax (770) 914-5976

December 14, 2004

Dr. Paul Chappell
Lancaster Baptist Church
4020 East Lancaster Boulevard
Lancaster, CA 93535

Dear Bro. Chappell:

I cannot tell you how much Trish and I enjoyed our recent trip to California. We always love spending time with you and Terrie, and this was no exception. The time spent with the other pastors and their wives was such a refreshing time for us, as well.

As you know, sometimes pastors need time away to be ministered to—and those days were perfect for us. We enjoyed the sessions, and we learned a wealth of ideas to help with our ministry here. We came back inspired and excited about what the Lord has in store for us.

Thank you so much for everything: the accommodations, the wonderful meals, and the invitation to come. You and your people were so kind and generous. It was all greatly appreciated.

I consider you a dear friend and mentor. Thank you for the blessing you have been to me. If there is ever any way I can be a help to you, please do not hesitate to call.

Sincerely,

David A. McCoy

*It Pays to Serve God!*
PSALM 84:11

*Trinity*

February 1, 1996

Pastor Paul Chappell
Lancaster Baptist Church
4020 E. Lancaster Blvd.
Lancaster, CA 93535

Dear Bro. Chappell:

Congratulations on your 10th anniversary as pastor at the Lancaster Baptist Church. Truly the work that God has raised up under your leadership there in Southern California has a testimony that is known around the world. I appreciate so much your strong leadership and the vision that God has given to you to lead that great ministry.

Not only do I count you as a great leader in the independent Baptist movement but it's my privilege to count you as a dear personal friend. I thank God for your refreshing spirit, your God sized vision and your dedication to the Lord Jesus Christ. You and your family have been used of God to be a blessing to so many people. I trust that God gives you many more years of great ministry as you seek to impact the world through the ministries at Lancaster. Thank you for allowing me to have a small part in what God is using you to do in a great way. I trust God continues to pour out His blessings upon the great ministry and the wonderful people there at Lancaster.

In His Service,

Tom Messer

Tom Messer

TM:ifh

# FIRST BAPTIST CHURCH

Box 274 • 2440 King Road
Bridgeport, Michigan 48722

(517) 777-0210

R.B. Ouellette, *Pastor*
Bill Swain, *Assistant*
Roger Powell, *Assistant*
Brad Dalton, *Assistant*
Rick Dressler, *Assistant*

January 15, 1996

Pastor Paul Chappell
Lancaster Baptist Church
4020 E. Lancaster Blvd.
Lancaster, CA 93535

Dear Brother Chappell,

Congratulations on ten years of ministry at Lancaster Baptist Church!

I do not know if a church has ever had a better beginning decade of ministry than you and the good folks at Lancaster Baptist have enjoyed. You are to be commended, my Brother, for your vision, your diligence, your consistency, your faithfulness to the Word of God, and your exceptionally hard work.

Not only have you been a blessing to the people of your church and your community, but you have been an example to preachers and churches all across America.

I am thoroughly persuaded that in the days ahead Lancaster Baptist Church will occupy the same position of leadership, greatness, and inspiration as Highland Park Baptist Church, Trinity Baptist Church of Jacksonville, Temple Baptist Church of Detroit, Akron Baptist Temple, Immanuel Baptist Church of Pontiac, and other great churches have enjoyed in the past.

I appreciate your friendship. I pray God will continue to bless and use you. I look forward to seeing your ministry expanded, your influence extended, and your leadership greatly enhanced. You have a great past and a greater future.

May this special time of celebration be the encouragement and honor that you deserve. God bless you.

Your Friend,

R.B. Ouellette, Pastor

*The Church That Cares About You*

# *First Baptist Church*
## OF BRIDGEPORT

R.B. OUELLETTE, PASTOR; BILL SWAIN, SCOTT COWLING, AARON WILSON, J.D. HOWELL: ASSISTANTS

July 24, 2006

Dr. Paul Chappell
Lancaster Baptist Church
4020 E Lancaster Blvd
Lancaster CA 93535

Dear Brother Chappell,

What a meeting! I do not know if I've ever been in a better meeting in my life: inspiration, encouragement, instruction, laughter, tears, enthusiasm, but most of all, the hand of God. I was so impressed at the over-arching theme of depending and relying on God; being led by Him and serving for Him. This emphasis of course is always much needed in our lives, but especially so in this new era of fundamentalism.

My Brother, I believe God is using you to set a new model and forge a new path for this generation of fundamentalism: one that appreciates man, but worships God; one that honors leaders, but serves the Lord; one that is open and honest, willing to receive counsel and guidance, and yet ultimately committed to doing the will of the Lord.

I am so glad I got to be a part of the week.

Thank you for your many kindnesses to me and my family while we were there. Thank you for the lovely, large room, the marvelous basket of goodies, and for the excellent host. ☺ Thank you for the very generous offering and for the time I got to fellowship with you at lunch. Thank you for letting me use your office to study.

Most of all, thank you for driving all the way from Lancaster to Canoga Park so we could have a meal and some fellowship together on Tuesday. What a great privilege and blessing that was.

I pray for you every day. I believe God is only going to use you in a greater and greater way as time goes on. Thank you again for everything, but most of all for being my friend. God bless you.

Your Friend,

R.B. Ouellette, Pastor

# First Baptist Church
## OF BRIDGEPORT

R.B. Ouellette, Pastor; Scott Cowling, Aaron Wilson, J.D. Howell: Assistants

July 23, 2009

Dr. Paul Chappell
Lancaster Baptist Church
4020 E. Lancaster Blvd.
Lancaster, CA 93535

Dear Dr. Chappell,

Thank you for the privilege of preaching at Lancaster Baptist Church on Sunday and at the Leadership Conference on Tuesday. What an honor! The conference was absolutely tremendous. The Spirit of God was obviously at work in the service and at the sessions. You are dong more to steer God's men in the right direction than anyone in Fundamentalism There can be no question but that you are the most influential leader in our movement and your church is the most followed example. Thanks for letting me be a small part of the great things God is using you to do.

Thank you, too, for keeping a Christ-like spirit, deflecting honor and praise to God, and being kind and compassionate to those who are on the other side of some issues. I think the tone of the conference was just right and agree with you that it was especially important this year that our primary emphasis be one of help and outreach rather than one of correction. Of course, I recognize that is always your general heart for the conference, but I felt you had a special burden for that this year and totally appreciate it.

Thank you for your many kindnesses to me. Thank you for the very generous love offering, thank you for the nice room and the basket of goodies in Lancaster. Thank you especially for the great time of fellowship with you and Terry after the meeting. I enjoyed the Dodgers game and was in awe of our accommodations in Laguna Beach. Thank you for taking so much time to fellowship with Krisy and me. It was a real treat.

I look forward to seeing you at the Sword. Please call me any time I can be of any help or encouragement to you. I pray for you daily and deeply appreciate the opportunity to minister with you. God bless you.

Your Friend,

R. B. Ouellette
Pastor

# FIRST BAPTIST CHURCH

*THE CHURCH THAT CARES ABOUT YOU*

*- PASTOR R.B. OUELLETTE*

July 26, 2010

Dr. Paul Chappell
Lancaster Baptist Church
4020 E Lancaster Blvd
Lancaster CA 93535

Dear Dr. Chappell,

What an awesome conference! I'm so sorry that I was able to be there for only a slice of it. I was indeed thrilled, encouraged, and uplifted by the little bit that I saw.

Your preaching Monday night was phenomenal. I have never heard you better.

From what I could see the emphasis of the conference was just right. Though I appreciate and share your heart to avoid unnecessary controversy and not be an "issues meeting," I think that our current situation required that a strong yet encouraging voice be lifted. You certainly provided that in the meeting.

I've heard many good reports about the meeting and look forward to hearing more of the sessions on line as I begin to dig out from my wedding activities and events.

I don't know if I'll get to see you at the Sword conference or not, but I sure look forward to being with you in August. Thanks again for all of your love, kindness, and attention. The room was lovely, the basket was excellent, the many gifts of books, CD's, and other material were overwhelming, and I thoroughly enjoyed the privilege of preaching at such a great meeting.

I appreciate your friendship and pray daily for you as you exercise such leadership for the cause of Christ. God bless you.

Your Friend,

R.B. Ouellette, Pastor

RBO/lh

---

2400 King Rd., Saginaw, MI 48601    Tel.: 989-777-0210    Email: fbcbridgeport@sbcglobal.net
P.O. Box 249, Bridgeport, MI 48722    Fax: 989-777-7376    Web: www.2fbc.com

# *RIVERVIEW BAPTIST CHURCH*

Home of Riverview Baptist Christian Schools
(Kindergarten through Twelfth Grade)
**Christian Family Radio—KOLU 90.1 FM**
P.O. Box 2734 ~ 4921 W. Wernett ~ Pasco, WA 99301
Church Phone (509) 547-2021

**Dr. John Paisley,** *Pastor*        **Dr. Ken Griffin,** *Co-Pastor*

July 31, 2009

Dr. Paul Chappell
Lancaster Baptist Church
4020 E. Lancaster Blvd.
Lancaster, CA 93535

Dear Bro. Paul,

I'm writing to thank you and the Lord for a blessed week at the recent Leadership Conference. The music and the messages were so challenging to my heart. Thank you for asking me to share the burden of my heart through hurts, and especially thank you for the Soldier of Grace award that you totally surprised me with on Tuesday night!

I'm always blessed every time I come to the college to speak and especially blessed with my first leadership conference. Thank you for your burden for people going to hell and what you are doing to reach these people. I'm so grateful for your wonderful discipleship follow up program you have there at the church.

I enjoyed seeing your dad and mom again and meeting the many new brethren I've not had the privilege of meeting before. It was sweet fellowship.

I keep saying thank you, but thank you for the generous love offering, and thank you most of all for your fellowship and love.

Love in Christ,

Bro. Paisley

July 30, 2010

Dear Dr. Chappell,

Thank you again for bringing me out to Lancaster Baptist Church. It was a "never-to-be-forgotten" memory. And again thank you for letting me bring Jonathan. You were so kind to give us the books and Bibles with our names imprinted. You treated us like royalty.

By the way, our Assistant Pastor has returned from the Spiritual Leadership Conference a changed man (for good!)! Thank you for all you've done for America! I love you! Forever friends,

Johnny Pope

Johnny Pope

June 6, 2007

Dr. Paul Chappell
Lancaster Baptist Church
4020 East Lancaster Blvd.
Lancaster, CA 93535

Dear Brother Chappell,

Thank you for your note. Even though we knew for over a year, that Dr. Falwell would probably be taken home to be with his Lord and Saviour, it was still a sorrowful time. However we are not without hope.

As Chairman of the Board of Trustees of Liberty University, I am happy to report that Dr. Falwell lived long enough to see his dream come true; a World Class University. I am also happy to report that the University is debt-free and it's future without Dr. Falwell continues to look bright.

I rejoice over the great reports that I hear about your ministry. I am pleased to say that I know you personally.

Sincerely,

Jerry Prevo

---

Dr. Jerry Prevo, Pastor • 6401 E. Northern Lights Blvd. • Anchorage, Alaska 99504
T: 907.333.6535 • F: 907.929.9851 • www.ancbt.org

# Bible Baptist Church

1701 HARNS ROAD, OAK HARBOR, WASHINGTON 98277 U.S.A.

COMMITTED
TO THE NEXT
GENERATION

Office: (360) 675-8311
School: (360) 679-6497
Fax: (360) 240-8347
E-Mail: baptist@whidbey.net
Web: www.bbcoakharbor.org

**PASTORS**
Dr. Gary S. Prisk, *founder*
Robert J. Sargent

Jeremiah J. Sargent
*Minister to the pastors*

November 7, 2003

Dr. Paul Chappell
West Coast Baptist College
4020 E. Lancaster Blvd.
Lancaster, CA 93535

Dear Dr. Chappell,

Greetings in our Saviour's all sufficient grace.

I want to thank you again for inviting me to the college and allowing me the opportunity to invest in the lives of the students the Lord has placed there. It is a commitment to the next generation that is desperately needed at this hour. May the Lord strengthen you in your resolve to "equip them for the work of the ministry."

The opportunity to fellowship with you and your wife on Wednesday and Thursday evenings was refreshing. Thank you for your hospitality and care of me personally.

Be assured of my prayers concerning the burdens and challenges you shared with me.

On the easy side of the yoke,
Your friend,

Brother Prisk

Bible Baptist School (K–12) ● Pastors School Bible Institute ● Bible Baptist Church Publications ● Teen Impact Ministries
Mindanao Baptist Outreach ● Stanwood Baptist Outreach ● Nevada Baptist Outreach
Island County Jail Ministry ● Outreach to Single Military Personnel ● Rest Home Ministries ● Retirement Ministries

A Home for Your Family . . .

A Heart for Our World

October 4, 2007

Dr. Paul Chappell
Lancaster Baptist Church
4010 E. Lancaster Blvd.
Lancaster, CA 93535

Dear Brother Chappell,

Thank you so much for the opportunity to preach in the chapel service of West Coast Baptist College last week. It was indeed an honor and privilege. I pray that the Lord used the message in the lives of the students to encourage and challenge them.

Sharon and I also appreciate all the hospitality given to us during our brief stay. Thank you for the transportation both from and to the airport, the nice hotel room, the gift bags, the meals, the reimbursement of my airfare, and honorarium. It all added to our pleasant experience there.

We really appreciate you taking your time to take us to lunch on Tuesday as well. We enjoyed the meal and the opportunity to fellowship with you, Larry, and Ashley. I know that your schedule is full, but I enjoyed getting to know you better.

I also want you to know that the Lord has used you, your staff, and your ministry to be a blessing to me, my staff, and our church. I am looking forward to you and Dr. Ouellette being with us in February, 2009.

One thing that I was going to ask for while there was the flow chart of your staff that I asked about at the conference in South Carolina last month. Would you mind sending that to me?

Thanks again for everything.

Yours for Souls,

Tim Rabon
Pastor

TR/sr

2110 Trawick Road | Raleigh, NC 27604 | 919.872.2215 | www.ahomeforyourfamily.com
**Tim Rabon, Pastor**

# CORNERSTONE BAPTIST CHURCH

Terry L. Randolph, Pastor
James C. Gardner, Associate Pastor

4041 East Phelps,    Phoenix, Arizona 85032

(602) 867-2700

July 14, 1994


Pastor Paul Chappell
Lancaster Baptist Church
4020 E. Lancaster Blvd
Lancaster, Calif 93535

Dear Bro. Paul:

I want to write and personally thank you for inviting me to
your Eight Anniversary Celebration week.  I appreciated so
much the opportunity to attend the meetings Monday - Tuesday,
and once again, be given the privilege of visiting and fellow-
shipping with you.  I appreciated so much the preaching and
practical sessions, they were a great encourgement and personal
challege to me.  Every speaker, including yourself I felt did
an incredible job.  I also would like to thank you for all the
special things, like paying for my room, purchasing my supper,
providing breakfast, putting on the best lunch ever, the steak
was great!  And I personally enjoyed and appreciated the invite
to your home Tuesday Evening.  Please inform your wife that the
food was great and your home was beautiful.  I guess I could go
on and on with so many things, the basket of fruit in the room
that I realize was for the speaker, but I ate part of it too.
You truly are a very wonderful and gracious host.

I am very happy for your ministry and proud of you personally
for the great leadership you are providing for your church.
I thought one of the things that was so special, was the excitement and enthusiasm of your people, that truly added to a great
meeting.  I want you to know that I pray daily for you, that
God will continue to give you great wisdom, physical stamina,
and spiritual protection from the devil.  Thank you for being
such a good friend, and a great inspiration to me.


Your friend,

Terry L. Randolph

*Jesus Christ Himself Being the Chief Corner Stone. Ephesians 2:20*

# CORNERSTONE BAPTIST CHURCH

Terry L. Randolph, Pastor
James C. Gardner, Associate Pastor

4041 East Phelps,   Phoenix, Arizona 85032

(602) 867-2700

May 30, 1995

Pastor Paul Chappell
Lancaster Baptist Church
4020 E. Lancaster Blvd
Lancaster, CA 93535

Dear Bro. Paul,

I am so sorry you did not receive your picture of PC that I
mailed to you after graduation week.  Enclosed is another one
I had left over, I hope you enjoy it.

Let me say again how much I appreciate your prayers and financial
support to PC.  This has truly been a difficult year as you know
with all that has transpired.  I am so thankful for good men like
you, that I believe really has a geniune heart for the school to
see it succeed.  Your personal friendship and encouragement means
a great deal to me, and I am hoping that it will only continue to
be strengthened, through our mutual interest in the training of
men and women for the Gospel ministry.

I am looking forward with great antiscipation at coming to West
Coast in September and speaking in Chapel.  Thank you for inviting
me, as I will pray to be an encouragement to your students.  I
know that launching out to start a Bible College has been a great
undertaking for your church.  But I am confident of your character
and skills and know it will prove to be a wonderful school for the
glory of God.

Please let me know if there is anything I can do to be a help to
you, as it is in my heart also to see West Coast succeed.  I will
be talking with you again in the near future, just to confirm
things in September.  May God richly bless you, until He comes
again!

Sincerely,

Terry L. Randolph

mr

*Jesus Christ Himself Being the Chief Corner Stone. Ephesians 2:20*

# Faith Baptist Church and Schools

### Dr. Roland Rasmussen, Pastor

7644 Farralone Avenue, Canoga Park, California 91304    (818) 340-6131

September 28, 2000

Pastor Paul Chappell
Lancaster Baptist Church
4020 E. Lancaster Blvd.
Lancaster, CA  93535

Dear Brother Chappell,

It was very kind and considerate of you to send the large plant for my fortieth anniversary as pastor of Faith Baptist Church.

Thank you for your kindness and for being a blessing to Mark and his family.

In Christ,

*Roland Rasmussen*

Roland Rasmussen

# TIMOTHY R. RASMUSSEN

July 18, 2003

Dear Pastor Chappell,

Thank you for once again providing the Spiritual Leadership Conference as a place where Christian workers can come and be challenged, stirred, helped and refreshed.

It is wonderful to see what God is doing in Lancaster. I am thankful for the impact Lancaster Baptist Church and West Coast Baptist College have had in my life as well as in the lives of many of our young people.

God is using you and your staff in a most unbelievable way. Thank you for helping others.

Your friend,

Tim Rasmussen

7644 *Farralone Avenue* Canoga Park *California* 91304
Residence: 805-578-1804   Oficce: 818-340-6131, Ext. 213   E Mail: *timkelras@att.net*

# Faith Baptist Church and Schools

Dr. Roland Rasmussen, Pastor | Tim Rasmussen, Co-Pastor

May 11, 2010

Dr. Paul Chappell
Lancaster Baptist Church
4020 E Lancaster Blvd
Lancaster, CA 93535

Dear Pastor Chappell,

Thank you again for the great privilege to speak at the Spring Concert last night. I appreciated so much the delicious dinner, time spent with you and your family, and kind honorarium. I truly thank the Lord for you, your family, Lancaster Baptist Church, and West Coast Baptist College.

It is an honor to be your friend, and I am continuing to pray for you, the ministry there, and for Larry as he continues to recover.

Thank you once again for the kindness you have shown me.

Your friend,

Tim Rasmussen

Dr. Paul Chappell
Landcaster Baptist Church
4020 E. Landcaster Blvd.
Landcaster CA. 93535

Dear Brother Chappell,

I wanted you to know how much we all appreciated the Spiritual Leadership Conference! All the people I brought with me were helped, and better equipped afterward for the service of the Lord. Your church family was very kind and welcoming. All the meals were excellent. Your approach to ministry is very well balanced and so needed in this hour. Wendy and I were honored to be able to fellowship and dine with you and some of the brethren following the Monday evening service. I was able visit for a moment with Danielle as she took care of one of the book tables. She is a godly young lady and a credit to you and Terrie.

The Conference rekindled our fires and helped us to get back to soulwinning and discipling with renewed enthusiasm. Since we got back I have been used of God in Leading 7 folks to Christ, five adults and two teens. With others, we've seen about 15 saved in last 2 weeks. We have several lined up to baptize Sunday.

I'm thankful to the Lord for you and your family's friendship, and looking forward to great things while it is yet day.

Best regards,

Bill Rench
Pastor
Calvary Baptist Church

**Calvary Baptist Church**
31087 Nicolas Road, Temecula, CA 92591
(909) 676-8700 Fax (909) 693-3226 E-mail calbaptem@juno.com
**Wm. Rench, Pastor**

*Contending for truth, not traditions or trends*

**Gospel Light Baptist Church**

Bobby Roberson
Pastor

P. O. Box 38 Walkertown, NC 27051
Church Phone (336) 722-9700

Steve Roberson
Co Pastor

September 10, 1999

Dr. Paul Chappell
Lancaster Baptist Church
4020 E. Lancaster Blvd.
Lancaster, CA 93535

Dear Bro. Paul:

Words cannot express my appreciation for you letting me preach in your church. You are always so nice and kind to me.

Thank you so much for the nice motel room, the fruit basket, and all of the goodies. You went out of your way to help me bring the basket home. Please thank your people for all the kind deeds; the peaches, the tomato sandwiches, etc. Thank you also for the nice honorarium.

As you know, you have some wonderful people. As I have said before, I do not know of any church in America that God has His hand on like Lancaster Baptist. My prayer is that God will continue to bless you and that He will give you wisdom to lead your people.

Please thank Terri for the good meal that we enjoyed in your home, and tell the children hello for me. I hope our paths cross in the near future, and maybe we can have you again at Gospel Light in the future. Keep standing true, and pray for us.

In Christ,

Bobby Roberson

BR:mb

# *Pleasant Valley Baptist Church*

*"The only difference about us is . . . we haven't changed."*

February 3, 1999

Dr. Paul Chappell
Lancaster Baptist Church
4020 E Lancaster Blvd.
Lancaster, CA 93535

Dear Bro. Chappell,

Just wanted to write a note to let you know that I'm looking forward to our meetings on the 22nd and 23rd. Not only am I personally looking forward to hearing the messages that God has laid upon your heart, but I am also looking forward to the fellowship. I hope I have it worked out so you can bring your wife and family. That would be just awesome. I sure would like to make this a two way street — you being a blessing to us and likewise we being a blessing to you.

Bro. Chappell, if you would take the liberty to talk about the college at length, it would be much appreciated. I believe we will have six to eight students going to West Coast Baptist College this coming year. After much, much prayer, I have asked my son, Gabriel to attend West Coast Baptist College. I honestly believe that's God's will for his life for his training for the ministry. He's my oldest son, Bro. Chappell. I did not take this decision lightly. I sincerely want the best for him. I believe that's exactly where he will get it.

So, I'm looking forward to seeing you soon. Enclosed is a check to help with any miscellaneous things you might need to make the trip. Hope it's a blessing to you. God bless you, buddy.

Your friend,

Pastor Tim Ruhl

*Three Fifty-five Panama Ave.* ✦ *Chico, California 95973*
*Church (530) 343-0555* ✦ *Schools (530) 343-2949* ✦ *Fax (530) 343-0758*
*Tim Ruhl, Pastor*

# Pleasant Valley Baptist Church
*"The only difference about us is . . . we haven't changed."*

July 24, 2002

Bro. Paul Chappell
Lancaster Baptist Church
4020 E Lancaster Blvd.
Lancaster, CA 93535

Dear Bro. Chappell,

Thank you so much for the tremendous help from this year's Leadership Conference. I also wanted to thank you for the kind gifts that were in the registration packet. I am looking forward to listening to the message "Behold the Lamb of God."

Bro. Chappell, I know I wrote you a note on Tuesday morning, but I just wanted to reiterate how much I appreciated the message Monday night. It was definitely of God. I guess the reason that I enjoyed it so much was that I was able to watch my dear friend be used of the Lord in such a great way. As in context, you were definitely burning and shining. I loved it. Even when God looked down and saw His Son following in obedience of baptism, He said, "This is my beloved Son in Whom I am well pleased." I feel I could say the same — "That's my dear friend who's doing a great job preaching and I am so pleased." I think the reason we have such a great friendship is because we have found security in the Lord in our own ways. I'm not a threat to you. I'm not in competition. We both tremendously realize we are on the same team. Thanks for hitting a home run. Thanks for scoring a touchdown. Thanks for being used of God. I enjoyed cheering you on that night.

I am praying for the sequester event. I am also praying to be a help to your brother, Steve. I look forward to seeing you soon. I will have to come down to West Coast Baptist College and threaten all the guys when I drop my daughter off. Hey, Bro. Chappell, I love you. Have a great day.

Your friend,

Pastor Tim Ruhl

13539 Garner Lane ✦ Chico, California 95973
Church (530) 343-0555 ✦ Schools (530) 343-2949 ✦ Fax (530) 894-7823
Tim Ruhl, Pastor

## PLEASANT VALLEY BAPTIST CHURCH

"Teaching them to observe all things whatsoever I have commanded you: and, lo,
I am with you alway, even unto the end of the world." – Matthew 28:20

July 6, 2007

Bro. Chappell,

I just wanted to write a few words to say thank you so much for the wonderful opportunity to preach at Lancaster Baptist Church on a Wednesday night service and then to preach another year at the Men and Boys' Campout. I know I have already said it once before, but the highlight of the trip is just traveling up together. I am certainly appreciate those few hours of fellowship and conversation and seeking to do more for the Savior. It's always a great time.

Bro. Chappell, I am so proud of Larry. He seems to have adapted to married life well with a great vision ahead of him. How we can say like John, "I have no greater joy than to see my children walk in truth."

Thank you for the accommodations, the day with Maggie, and the very generous love offering. I have been praying for the Leadership Conference. I pray all goes well. Thank you again for your friendship, your kindness, and most of all, your example as you walk with God.

Your buddy,

Pastor Tim Ruhl

**Pleasant Valley Baptist Church** • 13539 Garner Lane
Chico, CA 95973 • Phone (530) 343-0555 • Fax (530) 343-0758
Tim Ruhl, Pastor • www.pvbaptist.org

# WITH GOD ALL THINGS ARE POSSIBLE
### PLEASANT VALLEY BAPTIST CHURCH

November 26, 2008

Dear Bro. and Mrs. Chappell,

I just wanted to write a note to say thank you so much for the very generous Thanksgiving gift. Wow, what a blessing! Just as the Bible says good news from a far country blesses the soul, so thoughts and acts of kindness such as this gift. My wife and I think the world of the two of you. We enjoy every moment we get to spend together. I'm sorry it is not as often as we would like.

We sure are proud of what God has accomplished through the both of you. Praise the Lord. Only Heaven will really show what the true reward is. Thanks for being faithful. Thanks for being our friends. Most of all, thanks for just being who you are. We love you folks.

Your friends,

Pastor and Mrs. Ruhl

*But Jesus beheld them, and said unto them, With men this is impossible; but **with God all things are possible**. —*MATTHEW 19:26

13539 Garner Lane | Chico, California 95973 | 530.343.0555 | pvbaptist.org | Tim Ruhl, Pastor

# PASTORS S–Z

# Montecito Baptist Church

### Dr. Ezekiel Salazar, Pastor

July, 18 2003

Dr. Paul Chappell
Lancaster Baptist Church
4020 E. Lancaster Blvd.
Lancaster, CA 93535

Dear Bro. Chappell,

I imagine that after a week of incredible blessing your cup is full and running over. The presence of the Holy Spirit of God was key to making the meeting what it turned out to be. It is obvious that Godly living and much prayer was invested for the conference.

I particularly wanted to thank you for all the sessions that were given by you for senior pastors. I was refreshed, reminded and encouraged to continue to serve and love my people.

I don't know if this is so. But I believe that the true reason why you invited me to speak in the sessions was so that I could attend to the conference. Thank you very much for the honor you gave me to be there. Than you for the beautiful hotel room, the wonderful service you gave to my family and the more than generous love offering. I love you and will continue to pray for you.

Continue to pray for us as we take the next step for the Lord. Than you for everything you have done for me personally and for my church.

Your Servant,

Dr. Ezequiel Salazar Jr.
Pastor

*2560 Archibald Ave., Ontario, Ca. 91761 (909) 923-8455*

# Montecito Baptist Church

*" 25 Years of Grace "*
*1979-2004*

March 11, 2004

Dr. Ezekiel Salazar Jr.
**Pastor**

Jose Pineda
**Assistant Pastor**

Miguel De Anda
**Youth Pastor**

Gary Blumer
**School Principal**

Milton Granados
**Finance Manager**

*25 Year*

*Silver*

*Anniversary*

2560 Archibald Ave.
Ontario, CA 91716
(909) 923-8455

Dr. Paul Chappell
Lancaster Baptist Church
4020 E. Lancaster Blvd.
Lancaster, CA 93535

Dear Brother Chappell:

It was so good to see you this last week at the fine arts competition. As always, your staff did an excellent job.

I just finished listening to your CD on the Spirit Filled Pastor. As I listened, I wept knowing the great need that I have for the Holy Spirit of God to be in control of my life. There are many men in our country who are so different in the way they run their ministries. But there is one obvious common denominator in every one of them, the hand of God is on their life.

Once again, thank you for being my friend, thank you for living a life led of the Spirit, which makes you a true friend. I pray for you, please continue to pray for us.

Your servant,

Ezekiel Salazar
Pastor

*Heritage*
BAPTIST CHURCH

11 May 2005

Dear Paul:

Just a note to Congratulate you on your 10th year commencement. I would have loved to be with you.

I think and pray for you often, you are a dear LONG DISTANT friend. I love you.

Sincerely,
Bro. Schearer

P.S. If I can do anything for you, Please do not hesitate to Call.     406-899-2810 cel

~Montana's Friendliest Church ~ Dr. S.C. Schearer, Pastor~

Mailing Address: PO Box 2002  Great Falls, MT  59403 ~ Church Address: 900-52nd Street North  Great Falls, MT
Church 406-454-2028 ~ Fax 406-454-2025 ~ Heritage Baptist School 406-454-2333 ~ Pastor's Cellular 406-899-2510

Serving the King

# TEMPLE BAPTIST CHURCH

CLARENCE SEXTON, PASTOR

October 3, 1994

Pastor Paul Chappell
Lancaster Baptist Church
4020 E. Lancaster Blvd.
Lancaster, CA 93535

Dear Brother Paul:

Evelyn and I want to thank you for every kindness shown us on our recent trip. We had no idea that you and Terrie would be willing to spend the kind of time with us that you spent.

For years, I have heard good things about your ministry. The truth is, the half has never been told. God is doing mighty things through your life.

I deeply appreciate the generous love gift, the delicious meals, and most importantly, you folks giving of yourselves. The Lord Jesus Christ could not have been treated better in Bethany than I was treated in Lancaster.

May God continue to bless and use you, your family, your outstanding church staff, and the precious people at Lancaster Baptist Church.

Thank you for your friendship.

Yours in Christ,

Clarence Sexton

Acts 5:42

CS:aw

P.S. I am sending some Crown College information under separate cover. Perhaps you can pass it along to your school folks.

BEAVER CREEK AT ADAMS ROAD ♦ PO BOX 159 ♦ POWELL TN ♦ 37849
615 ♦ 938-8182 ♦ FAX: 615 ♦ 938-8188

Serving the King

# TEMPLE BAPTIST CHURCH

CLARENCE SEXTON, PASTOR

August 30, 1995

Dr. Paul Chappell
Lancaster Baptist Church
4020 E. Lancaster Boulevard
Lancaster, CA 93535

Dear Brother Paul:

Rarely does one pastor have the opportunity to see the heart of another pastor's ministry. Thank you for inviting us into your heart. I want to be worthy of your trust. We enjoyed every minute of the retreat and the church and college meeting. I learned so very much from observing your ministry.

Thank you for the lovely places to stay and the delicious meals, especially the In and Out Burgers--praise the Lord! I am extremely grateful for the very generous love gift.

Evelyn and I love you and Terrie. We deeply appreciate your friendship. You have a wonderful family and a wonderful work.

May God continue to bless and use you. Please give my warmest regards to your family. Stay in touch.

Yours in Christ,

Clarence Sexton

CS:aw

P.S.  When you get out our way, we will talk more about the Christian leadership idea.

Clarence Sexton

Dec. 22, 2009

Dear Paul & Terrie,

We are all very concerned and earnestly praying for Larry's healing. God is with you and many thousands of people are praying across the country and around the world.

Yours In Christ

Clarence Sexton

Acts 5:42

1700 Beaver Creek Drive • Powell, Tennessee 37849

# HARVEST BAPTIST CHURCH

884 Kenneth Avenue • New Kensington, PA 15068  724-337-0607 • 724-337-7794

**Kurt W. Skelly**
Pastor

**Charlie G. Rousey**
Asst. Pastor

**Ministries**
Academy
Bus
Junior Church
Missions
Nursery
Nursing Home
Soulwinning
Sunday School
Teen Group

February 19, 2003

Dr. Paul Chappell
Pastor
Lancaster Baptist Church
4020 East Lancaster Boulevard
Lancaster, CA 93535

Dear Dr. Chappell,

Please accept my sincerest gratitude for the gracious way by which you hosted our group and me this past week. Ostensibly I came to be a blessing to you but found that, in reality, *you* were a tremendous blessing to *me*.

At the risk of sounding patronizing, I want to thank you for your hospitality and spirit. I found our conversations to be informative, engaging, and refreshing. Thank you for your keen ability to maintain fundamental distinctions within the parameters of *grace* and for teaching others that these ideas need not be mutually exclusive.

It appears as if our group agrees with my review. As of now, all three of our young people who visited are making plans to attend West Coast Baptist College. Thank you for helping us help them. For what it is worth, I remain available to help in whatever capacity you need.

Please convey to Terrie and your children my heartfelt appreciation for their servant's spirit, and let them know that they certainly had an impact on my life.

Finally, and sincerely, please know that I will be praying for you and your ministry that God would bless you with all spiritual blessings in Christ Jesus.

Sincerely,

Kurt W. Skelly
Pastor

KWS:sg

*"That His Glory May Shine"*

200

# Kurt W. Skelly, Pastor

Harvest Baptist Church
884 Kenneth Avenue
New Kensington, PA 15068
724-337-0607

**Ministries**
Academy
Bus Ministry
Deaf Ministry
Detention Center Ministry
Helping Hands Ministry
High Rise Ministry
Hope Ministry
Junior Church
King's Kids
Ladies Missionary Group
Light of Life Mission Ministry
Missions
Nursery
Nursing Home Ministry
Reaching Others Ministry
Singles Ministry
Soulwinning
Sunday School
Teen Group
Veterans Ministry

April 15, 2005

Pastor Paul Chappell
Lancaster Baptist Church
4010 East Lancaster Boulevard
Lancaster, CA 93535

Dear Bro. Chappell,

Thank you for including me in the Youth Conference this year. I certainly do not take for granted your invitation, and I hope that everything met your expectations.

It has been one of the distinct joys of my ministry to be able to culture a friendship with you. I want you to know that I pray for you daily and consider you to be a trusted mentor in my life. Thank you for investing a part of yourself in people like me outside of the scope of your immediate family and church.

I'm looking forward to attending Leadership Conference this year, and I know that our people will be the beneficiaries for having attended with me.

My wife and children were overwhelmed by your tokens of generosity (gift cards to Target and Toy Warehouse). Thanks for being such a blessing!

Sincerely,

Bro. Skelly

Kurt W. Skelly
Pastor

KWS:sg

**Harvest Baptist**
m i n i s t r i e s

Planting. Watering. Reaping.

July 24, 2006

Pastor Paul Chappell
Lancaster Baptist Church
4010 East Lancaster Boulevard
Lancaster, CA 93535

Dear Bro. Chappell,

I want to thank you for allowing me to be a part of the Leadership
Conference this year. I planned to attend anyway, but the fact that you
included me as a speaker in the sessions was just an added bonus.
Thank you for having that confidence in me.

May I say how privileged I feel to be a part of anything that's going on
there at Lancaster Baptist Church. You folks certainly exhibit the spirit
of excellence in all that you say and do, and I was once again convicted
as I sat through the sessions and listened to the marvelous preaching.

Thank you, Bro. Chappell, for allowing God to use you in the ways that
He has. You are certainly a choice servant of God, and I thank Him for
allowing me to rub shoulders with you in the ways that I have.

I'm praying for you, my friend, that God would bless you, strengthen
you, and keep you in these days that lie ahead. Once again, thank you
for all of your kindnesses toward me. The accommodations, fruit
basket, fellowship, and love offering were above and beyond.

God bless you richly!

Sincerely,

Kurt W. Skelly
Pastor

KWS:sg

884 Kenneth Avenue  |  New Kensington, PA 15068  |  724.337.0607  |  www.harvestbaptist.info

**Kurt W. Skelly - Pastor**

# Faith Baptist Church

## And Christian Academy

5714 29th St. NE, Tacoma, WA 98422, Phone (253) 927-7673, FAX (253) 927-6062

October 11, 2000

Dr. Paul Chappell
Lancaster Baptist Church
4020 E Lancaster Blvd
Lancaster, CA 93535

Dear Bro. Chappell:

Just a personal note to say thank you for the privilege of speaking to the wonderful crowd of people who made Founder's Night so special for us all. To be a "partner in ministry" with you is a privilege we do not take lightly. We are concerned regarding whom and how we influence people for West Coast Baptist College, and we are thrilled for every student and every church that had gotten involved because of some small influence on our part.

We truly enjoyed ourselves at the meeting in spite of some setbacks. We appreciate the help with the suit, and we tried to return the love offering lest we add to the burden of the college. We managed to get away with the airfare, but they returned the offering, thanks for your graciousness. We enjoyed unity with you and sharing thoughts about the possibilities! We really appreciate your letting us stay with Leo & Evelyn and we hope we are an encouragement to them; they certainly are to us.

We were so grateful you allowed Bro. & Sister Ferrso to come and we hope they enjoyed their time here. We really wanted to let them see the Northwest and have a day or two to rest. Bro. Ferrso did a wonderful job preaching to our men and we had a great time of fellowship and challenge. We were also thankful for Mrs. Ferrso sharing some great insights with our pianists and she was so encouraging to our office staff.

We just can't thank you enough for investing in Faith and for helping us to keep growing for God! We are praying for you and for Bro. Goetsch and our heart's desire is that together we can see our greatest ever Missions Conference. We need to constantly renew our vision and see through His eyes! We are praying for your harvest month and count on your prayers as well. Hope to see you soon.

Love,

Bro. Mark
Col. 4:17

MTS/rk

Pastor Mark T. Smith

# Faith Baptist Church

### And Christian Academy

5714 29th St. NE, Tacoma, WA 98422, Phone (253) 927-7673, FAX (253) 927-6062

January 25, 2002

Dr. Paul Chappell, Pastor
Lancaster Baptist Church
4020 E. Lancaster Blvd.
Lancaster, California 93535

Dear Brother Chappell:

Just a note to personally thank you for coming as a guest speaker to Preacher's
Delight 2002, and for your kind words of encouragement, your friendship and your
counsel. We also appreciate your willingness to present the college ministry, Truth
for Today Publications and the Leadership Conference materials. We realize the
schedule is hectic and it is difficult to deal with the deluge of pastors, missionaries
and lay people who need your attention, but you appeared very gracious and
certainly very helpful.

We have already planned for you and Mrs. Terrie to join us next year and we
appreciate your willingness to come. Brother Gibbs plans to bring Glorianne as well
and we will have special accommodations arranged for all of our guest speakers. We
are especially grateful for your being a part of our first meeting in the new building
as well as the old building and, Lord-willing, the next building!

Thanks again for your friendship, your counsel and your influence. If we can be of
any help on your building projects with the college, please feel free to ask. As
always, count us your friends for Christ's sake.

Sincerely Serving the Savior,

Mark T. Smith
Col. 4:17

MTS:js

Enclosures:     New Beginnings Tract
                Pulpit Chronicles Letter

Pastor Mark T. Smith

# FIRST BAPTIST CHURCH

2970 Santa Maria Way, Santa Maria, California 93455

Phone: (805) 937-8405

*Dr. John E. Stevens, Pastor*
*Brian E. Barber, Assistant Pastor*
*Jay Cawthorn, Visitation Pastor*
*Paul Newlove, Discipleship Pastor*
*Mike Gessaro, Children's Pastor*
*Charles R. Mason, Principal-Administrator*
*Dan S. Spencer, High School Principal*

July 10, 1986

Pastor Paul Chappell
c/o Lancaster Baptist Church
304 W. Lancaster Blvd.
Lancaster, California 93534

Dear Brother Paul:

Greetings in the name of Him Who is all sufficient, even our Lord Jesus Christ! I am rejoicing over the fact that you have accepted the call to pastor there in Lancaster. I am sure it is going to be a tremendous struggle but I know that you are the man to do it. I am, also, praying that Brother Ormsby will be of some help to you.

I am sorry that I will not be able to help you on a regular monthly basis but please keep me posted as I am sure that we will want to do something from time to time.

May God richly bless you, my brother.

Your servant in Christ,

Dr. John E. Stevens
Pastor

JES/be

*"We Preach the Old Book, the New Birth, and the Blessed Hope"*

**Bible Baptist CHURCH**

*32 Park Avenue   St. Thomas, Ontario   Canada   N5R 4W1*
*Tel 519.631.3421   Fax 519.631.4917*

December 1, 2005

Dr. Paul Chappell
Lancaster Baptist Church
4020 E. Lancaster Blvd.
Lancaster CA 93535

Dear Bro. Chappell,

Thank you SO much for you note of encouragement.  It's always a blessing to know that others are thinking of you.  I don't write as often as I should but I want you to know that with each piece of literature that I get from Lancaster I do take time to think of you and thank the Lord for you and your wide spread ministry.

I have always enjoyed my times in Lancaster.  What a thrill it's been to be able to speak to the young people and college students there at Lancaster Baptist.

I wanted to thank you for the recognition you gave to my father-in-law this year.  The beautiful award that you presented him adorns the end table in their living room.

I pray that our paths will again cross soon.  I am hoping, Lord willing to be able to come to the leadership conference this year if all goes as planned.  We hope to be putting a shovel in the ground this spring for a Bearing Precious Seed Canada production and office facility.  Construction can make liars out of preachers, but I trust not this time.

My best to your staff and family!

A servant of the Saviour in St. Thomas.

Al Stone

Dr. Al Stone, *Pastor*
Pastor@CanadaBBC.org

Mike Hollen, *Associate Pastor*
PastorHollen@CanadaBBC.org
www.CanadaBBC.org
www.BPScanada.org

# Liberty Baptist Church of Las Vegas

**6501 WEST LAKE MEAD BLVD. ● LAS VEGAS, NEVADA 89108**
**702-647-4522**

*October 4, 1995*

*Dear Brother Chappell,*

*I wanted to write you and tell you that I enjoyed speaking to you the other day on the phone and appreciate your willingness to share with me all that you did about your desires for West Coast Baptist College and your philosophy in the area of Baptist history, separation and moral purity. My biggest concern in any ministry that we support is doctrinal purity and moral purity. I realize on some issues there will always be differences of opinion, even amongst fundamentalist. It is my concern, however, that the fundamentals of the faith be not just preached but lived and that Biblical morality be held in high esteem. Obviously, you intend to do that with West Coast Baptist College.*

*I admire what you have done in Lancaster and I want to be part of the college ministry. We are going to add you to our missions budget at $100 per month. You will also be added to our prayer list and we will be praying for God to bless you there at West Coast. God bless you Brother Chappell.*

*In His Service,*

*Dave Teis*
*Pastor*

*DMT:kp*

## Liberty Baptist Church

Pastor David Teis   6501 W. Lake Mead Blvd.  Las Vegas, NV 89108   702.647.4522   experienceliberty.com

January 17, 2008

Dr. Paul Chappell
Lancaster Baptist Church
4020 E. Lancaster Blvd.
Lancaster, CA 93535

Dear Brother Chappell,

I just received your note today. I wanted you to know that I thank God for you as well. There are very few people I pray for on a daily basis but you are one of them. I know that Satan is doing all he can to discourage you, but I also know that the power of God rests upon you and that God is able.

I'd like to thank you for so many things, the school, the example church that you have raised up, your friendship and for raising a godly daughter who has become my daughter's good friend. My prayer is that God will protect you and your family as you continue to serve Him. Please know that I am your friend and if there is anything I can ever do for you, you can contact me. I speak for the entire Teis family when I say we love you! God bless you!

In His Love,

Dave Teis

DMT:fet

# Bay View Baptist Church

22648 Grosenbach Road, Washington, IL 61571

## Pastor Keith D. Thibo

www.kingskidsclubs.org　　　　　　　　　　　　　　E-Mail: KeithThibo@yahoo.com

**Assistant Pastors**

Aaron Samples
Brett Bedwell

**Administrative Assistant**

Joe Mitchell

**Church Office**

Nancy Claypool
Sarah Johnson
Natasha Ellis

**Staff Evangelists**

Jim Reigle
David Anderson

**School Administrator**

Jon Kincaid

**King's Kids Int'l Baptist Mission**

Sheila Warren
Ken Claypool
Jim Blumenstock
Carlos Canamore
Charles Chandler

**Telephone**

(309) 698-2000

**FAX**

(309) 698-2065

May 9, 2007

Dr. Paul Chappell
West Coast Baptist College
4010 E. Lancaster
Lancaster, CA 93535

Dear Brother Chappell,

I trust that this letter finds you abounding in the grace and blessings of our LORD. It was wonderful to see you and the precious work God has given you. His hand of blessing is great upon you. Thank you for bringing me to West Coast Baptist College to preach and for the generous honorarium you provided.

Your students are very easy to preach to and I really enjoyed it. I pray that hearts were touched by the message. We are looking forward to your college summer team being with us in another month. May the LORD speak to the hearts of our young people concerning West Coast Baptist College. I would love to see them come your way.

Thank you also, for taking much time with me and the wonderful lunch we enjoyed together in your office. That time will become a part of my book of precious memories.

I'll stay in touch with you concerning things of ministry. God bless you. Thank you for your support. May we be found faithful until Jesus comes!

Sincerely Serving,

Keith D. Thibo
Pastor

## Illinois Central Christian School
### King's Kids International Baptist Mission

# EAST SIDE BAPTIST CHURCH

David Thomasson, Pastor

November 10, 2010

Dear Brother Chappell,

I would like to take this opportunity to thank you for the publications from Striving Together. In particular, I would like to thank you for the devotional book "The Daily Word". I have used this book each day for the last year. It has been a great help and it has been used to help me get in the mode for my Bible reading and pray time each day. In fact, I will be ordering a copy for each family in our church to give them on our Vision Night. I believe it will also be a great help to each of our families in our church and believe that they should have this.

I just wanted to send you a quick note just to let you know that once again that your ministry is being a great blessing to another ministry.

Thank you and may God bless you. We love you and your family and appreciate you very much. Have a great day.

Your Friend,

David Thomasson, Pastor

DT/mb

Your missionaries to Hong Kong:
## The DWIGHT TOMLINSON FAMILY
Eph. 5:16 †

P. O. Box 325-Sha Tin Central Post Office-Sha Tin, N. T., Hong Kong.

約
翰
福
音
三
章
十
六
節

神
愛
世
人

June 2, 1986

Dear Brother Ron,

I enjoyed very much talking with you and Tacy by telephone last week. Your entire family is very dear to me. We love you and do not cease to thank God for your friendship.

Regarding the items we discussed on the telephone, please be assured of my prayers for the church as they seek God's will concerning a new Pastor. You asked me about Paul Chappell. Everything I know about Paul Chappell and his wife is good. I have been extremely impressed by his sincerity and diligence in the Lord's work. He is young but he is not inexperienced. He has been around soul-winning churches all his life and has been a tremendous asset to the ministry at North Valley.

The more I think about Brother Chappell, the more I believe he deserves the church's prayerful consideration. He is a good man and he may be the man the Lord wants at R.B.C. I suggest you meet with him and discuss his doctrinal position, plans for building a church, family and financial relationships, etc., and at least give the Lord an opportunity to open or close the door.

Well brother, again, don't forget that we are praying for you. If there is any way at all that I can be of help to you during this critical time, don't hesitate to call me.

Your Friend and Co-worker,

Dwight Tomlinson

DRT/gt

Dear Paul,

Here is a copy of the letter I wrote to Ron Fleet, one of the deacons at R.B.C. I really have no control over their actions any longer but at least I can recommend — Good luck to you and may God lead & direct in your life to keep

Eph. 5:16 "Redeeming the time, because the days are evil."

you in the center of His will — I'm pulling for

211

you all the way. If there is anything I can
do for you—just drop me a note.
                    Your friend,

                    Dwight Fowler

# Liberty Baptist Church

5108 Bonita Canyon Drive, Irvine, CA 92715 (714) 854-9000 Dwight Tomlinson, Pastor

February 23, 1995

Paul Chappell
Lancaster Baptist Church
4020 E. Lancaster Blvd.
Lancaster, CA 93535

Dear Brother Chappell,

I have just received a letter that I believe to be an answer to prayer. It is the letter informing me of your decision to start a Bible college. It has been my conviction for many years that we must have the type of school you are planning to build. I believe you are the man that God has raised up for this hour in our state. Please accept my gratitude and complete support. I have no doubts that when WEST COAST BAPTIST COLLEGE opens its doors there will be students there from Liberty Baptist Church!

Sincerely,

Dwight Tomlinson

DT:dl

*a place to grow*

DWIGHT TOMLINSON

January 8, 2005

Dear Brother Chappell,

I wanted to say thank you for all the work that you put into advising me on the manuscript for the Missions book. I was surprised by how much thought and care you put into it. You are truly an amazing man! The more I am around you; the more I think I understand why God is using you in such a great way. You go the extra mile in everything you do. You redeem the time and make your life count for God. Thank you for being so wholeheartedly devoted to our Savior and to His people.

I count it a great honor to be your friend. As I said, the more I am around you the more impressed I am. You have not only impressed me though, you have also impacted me, for which I shall remain eternally grateful.

If there is ever anything I can do to be of service to you please let me know. I am indebted to you.

Your Friend in Him,

Dwight Tomlinson

*"...by love serve one another." Galatians 5:13*

LIBERTY BAPTIST CHURCH · 1000 BISON AVENUE · NEWPORT BEACH, CALIFORNIA 92660

BAPTIST CHURCH

September 5, 2007

Pastor Paul Chappell
Lancaster Baptist Church
4020 E Lancaster Blvd
Lancaster CA 93535

Dear Brother Chappell,

What an honor to be invited to participate in the special occasion in the life of your son, Larry. It was his grandfather, your father, Larry Chappell who ordained me more than thirty years ago!

I am so sorry that our Missions Conference is taking place that night. I am tempted to miss the Tuesday night of our conference but I don't think that would be right for me to do.

I must regretfully decline. If it had been the Tuesday before or after, I could have come but I cannot on Tuesday the 9th.

Please give my congratulations to Larry. What an excellent young man he has become! I know you are proud of him.

Sincerely,

Dwight Tomlinson

1000 Bison Avenue

Newport Beach

California 92660

949.760.5444

www.libertybaptistchurch.org

*Dwight Tomlinson,*

*Pastor*

*"If the Son therefore*

*shall make you free,*

*ye shall be free*

*indeed."* John 8:36

# North Valley Baptist Church
### of Santa Clara, California
### Nine Forty-One Clyde Avenue

October 18, 1988

Pastor Paul Chappell
Lancaster Baptist Church
304 W. Lancaster Blvd.
Lancaster, CA 93534

Dear Brother Chappell,

I wanted to write you a quick note and let you know how proud I am of you. It is very obvious to me and to preachers across our nation and especially in our state that you certainly have the power of God on your life. God has raised you up in these last days to do a tremendous work in the Lancaster area. However, I wanted to let you know that I believe your influence is going to reach far beyond Lancaster. Everywhere I go I make mention of the great work that you are doing. Presently I am in Arizona with Stan Slabaugh. He is a man of approximately my age, and he told me what a great influence you had on his life at the Pastors' Conference as you spoke about your work there in Lancaster and the work of God. Not only have you had influence on younger men and men my age, but certainly you have had an influence on my life. I believe God sent you my way several years ago to help define many areas of conviction, philosophy, etcetera. You are certainly a dear friend to me.

I also want to thank you for allowing me to have part in your ministry with your weekly telephone calls. I am always glad to hear that you are on the other end of the line. There are so many ways I look at you, Brother Chappell. I see you as a dear friend, a fellow pastor, as a wonderful example and teacher to me and others, as a younger brother. I guess mostly I see you as a man of God. Thank you for being a constant source of encouragement to me. God bless you.

Your Friend,

Dr. Jack A. Trieber
Pastor

JAT:pc

Dr. Jack A. Trieber, Pastor          Zip Code 95054          Telephone 408/988-8881

## North Valley Baptist Church
### of Santa Clara, California
### Nine Forty-One Clyde Avenue
### Zip Code 95054

April 15, 1991

Pastor Paul Chappell
Lancaster Baptist Church
304 W. Lancaster Blvd.
Lancaster, CA 93534

Dear Brother Chappell,

Thank you so much for providing such a nice evening and day for my wife and kids and myself at Stallion Springs. We certainly enjoyed our brief time together with you. Thank you for the hotel room, fruit basket, and both dinner and breakfast for me and my entire family. You are so very kind and thoughtful.

I also want to let you know what a real blessing it was just to be in your presence. You are always such an encouragement to me, Brother Chappell. Thank you for being my dear friend. I sure wish we weren't so many miles apart. It would certainly be fun to get together with you more often. You have a great way of encouraging me in the things of Christ. I certainly hope you know that I am proud of you. I am very proud of the great work that you have done there at Lancaster, and I am especially proud that you are preaching so many times at the First Baptist Church of Hammond this next week. What an honor to be able to fill the Wednesday night pulpit for Dr. Hyles in his absence. How thankful I am that they have you back there for the youth revival, and I want you to know that I will be praying for you as you preach these 16 messages this next week.

Thanks for being my dear friend and for always being an encouragement to me. God bless you.

Your friend,

Bro. Trieber

Dr. Jack A. Trieber
Pastor

JAT:pgc

Dr. Jack A. Trieber, Pastor     1975 Sweet Sixteen 1991     Telephone 408/988-8881

# North Valley Baptist Church

941 Clyde Ave Santa Clara, CA 95054
408/988-8881 Fax: 408/980-1400
Dr. Jack Trieber, Pastor

February 26, 1997

Dr. Paul Chappell
Lancaster Baptist Church
4020 E. Lancaster Blvd.
Lancaster, CA 93535

Dear Brother Chappell,

I just wanted to jot you a note and let you know that my heart is very heavy for you. I have been so sad today to hear the news that Jessica Downey was involved in this awful automobile accident. It is my prayer that by the time this letter is typed and received by you she will be on the road to recovery along with Elizabeth DeWitt.

As I am driving back to my home from Bakersfield tonight, my heart is so heavy. I want you to know that I have upheld you in prayer many times throughout the day and evening. I feel like your life has been like Job's. You are having this battle that you are suffering through along with some backslidden church members. In addition to that, there are a few pastors who feel like they sit in the seat of judgment as they analyze and scrutinize your ministry. I cannot help but think our Lord is allowing you to be tried so you can come forth as gold. Because of all these pressures and other pressures I know nothing about, I am asking our Lord to prove Himself more real to you than ever before, and I am asking Him to make it visible to the world so they can see that His hand is heavily upon you. You are a great man of God who has been an inspiration to me and to countless other preachers and thousands of God's people.

I trust you realize I truly love you and respect you and look up to you with great admiration. Please do not hesitate to call me if there is anything I can do to be a help to you, Brother Chappell. I want to seek to live my life to be a blessing to you. God bless you.

Your friend,

Dr. Jack Trieber
Pastor

JAT:pgc

# North Valley Baptist Church

### Dr. Jack Trieber, Pastor

Mailing Address:
3530 De La Cruz Boulevard
Santa Clara, California 95054

Church Location:
941 Clyde Avenue
Santa Clara, California 95054

August 18, 2003

Dear Dr. Chappell,

What an honor and delight it is to have you here with us for the next several days. I am thrilled for my staff and church family to have the opportunity to hear you teach and preach. I know that you will be a tremendous help and blessing to our ministry.

I am also extremely excited about the personal time that I will be able to spend with you and Larry while you are here. I count you as one of my dearest friends in the ministry, and thank God for the relationship He has allowed us to have.

I am so proud of all that God has used you to accomplish for his glory. You are a wonderful man, husband, father, pastor, preacher, leader, and personal friend. Your ministry in Lancaster is truly amazing. I cannot tell you how much I enjoyed my time with you and your staff last week. I was challenged, motivated, and inspired to do more for the cause of Christ here in Santa Clara because of my time spent with you.

If there is anything at all that I can do for you while you are here, please don't hesitate to let me know. I love you and am proud of you.

Your friend and co-laborer,

Pastor Trieber

JAT/rdt

# North Valley Baptist Church

### Dr. Jack Trieber, Pastor

Mailing Address:
3530 De La Cruz Boulevard
Santa Clara, California 95054

Church Location:
941 Clyde Avenue
Santa Clara, California 95054

August 26, 2005

Pastor Paul Chappell
Lancaster Baptist Church
4020 E. Lancaster Boulevard
Lancaster, CA 93535

Dear Bro. Chappell,

Greetings from our one-sided friendship! It seems as if I am always on the receiving end and hardly ever on the giving end of this friendship. I recently received three books from you in the mail. Several days before that, I received the book of Spurgeon's prayers. I had Bro. Harrell read a few of those prayers to my staff during Staff Orientation earlier this week. Thank you for always being so gracious and generous toward me.

My staff and I have been praying for you as you reopen the doors of your school for the fall semester. I have asked the men of our staff to pray that God would continue to bless not only your school this year but also your ministry in Lancaster. Thank you for being my dear friend, and thank you for being an encouragement to me. I respect you, look up to you, and greatly admire you. Thank you for all that you do for me. God bless you.

Your friend,

Bro. Trieber

JAT:cah

# Dr. Jack Trieber

### 3530 DE LA CRUZ BOULEVARD
### SANTA CLARA, CALIFORNIA 95054

July 30, 2007

Pastor Paul Chappell
Lancaster Baptist Church
4020 E. Lancaster Boulevard
Lancaster, CA 93535

Dear Bro. Chappell,

I received in the mail the book *Sending Forth Laborers* that you and Bro. Tomlinson wrote. Thank you for your thoughtfulness in sending me a copy! I am looking forward to reading this in the near future.

I also want to thank you for all that you are doing for the cause of Christ. Although it seems like we no longer talk on the phone together (my fault), I want you to know that I have your picture a short distance from my desk. In addition, I have the Chappell family picture on another shelf near my desk. They are constant reminders for me to pray for you.

I thank the Lord for you and admire all that you have accomplished for the King of kings. Thank you for your friendship. Please pray for me. God bless you.

Your friend,

Bro. Trieber

JAT:jge

# Dr. Jack Trieber

3530 DE LA CRUZ BOULEVARD

SANTA CLARA, CALIFORNIA 95054

September 20, 2010

Pastor and Mrs. Paul Chappell
Lancaster Baptist Church
4020 E. Lancaster Blvd.
Lancaster, CA 93535

Dear Bro. Chappell and Terrie,

You are amazing friends. Thank you for the beautiful flowers you sent us for our 25th anniversary of our Pastors' and Christian Workers' Conference. Thank you for your thoughtfulness. We are certainly enjoying the beauty of the various colors in this beautiful arrangement.

I also want to thank you for the tremendous testimony that you bear as you serve our Lord. Thank you for the way you have handled and are handling the physical situation of your dear son, Larry. Thank you, Terrie and Bro. Chappell, for being true to one another through these physical difficulties and hospitalization, even during the broken-bone experience with Danielle. Of course, I realize that these are just a few of the issues that you face on a day-by-day basis. Truly, your faith is spoken of throughout the whole world. Thank you for being great people. I love you dearly. God bless you.

Your friend,

Bro. Trieber

JAT/jge

# Bible Baptist Church

November 23, 2010

**Bible Baptist Church**

4190
Susquehanna Trail
North

York, PA 17404

Phone:
717.266.0892

Fax:
717.266.6718

Website:
www.bbcyork.com

Pastor:
Dr. Kevin E. Trout

Dear Brother Chappell,

I trust this letter finds you and your family doing well as we continue to pray for your son, Larry, and ask God's blessing on him and his life.

I just wanted to write you one more time and thank you for the extreme privilege it was to have you and Brother Ouellette here at our church for the Striving Together Conference.

It was one of the highlights of our ministry in the twenty-three years that we have been here. I do hold you in highest regard and believe you are one of the greatest leaders in America today.

I want you to know how much we love you and your ministry, Brother Chappell, and I am looking forward to coming out to preach at the college in December. I certainly do not deserve the privilege of doing so, but I appreciate the opportunity to come out there and see what the Lord is doing at West Coast Baptist College and Lancaster Baptist Church. It is a motivation to all of to keep on striving.

Once again, I thank you for coming to Bible Baptist.

Most esteemed,

Brother Trout

A FAMILY TO BE LOVED

**FALLS BAPTIST CHURCH**

For the Lord God is a sun and shield;
the Lord will give grace and glory;
no good thing will He withhold
from them that walk uprightly.
Psalm 84:11

July 12, 1989

Pastor
WAYNE VAN GELDEREN, JR.

Assistant to the Pastor
MIKE ASCHER

*Falls Baptist Academy*
Administrator
ROGER GAFKEN

Church Location
N69 W12703 APPLETON AVE.
MENOMONEE FALLS, WI
53051

414-251-7051

Mailing Address
P.O. BOX 164
MENOMONEE FALLS, WI
53051

Ministries
RADIO, BUS, DEAF,
YOUTH, JR. CHURCH,
COLLEGE & CAREER

Pastor Paul Chappell
Lancaster Baptist Church
304 W. Lancaster Boulevard
Lancaster, CA  93534

Dear Brother Chappell,

It certainly was a blessing having the opportunity to meet
you at the FBF meeting a few weeks ago.  I just wanted to
write and let you know how much I appreciated your session
on soulwinning.  It is refreshing to hear someone take a
strong, open stand about the need for winning folks to the
Lord.  I couldn't agree with you more in the emphasis that
you gave in your session.

I am sure we will continue to hear great things about your
ministry there in California.  I hope sometime in the future,
our paths will cross again.

God bless you!

In Christ,

Wayne Van Gelderen, Jr.

WVG/mm

224

# Fostoria Baptist Church

Robert E. Wall
*Pastor*

Todd Harrison
*Youth Pastor*

July 29, 2003

Dr. Paul Chappell
Lancaster Baptist Church
4020 E. Lancaster Blvd.
Lancaster, CA 93535

Dear Bro. Chappell,

Thank you for the tremendous Spiritual Leadership Conference. It met a real need in my life. My heart was stirred and I came home challenged to live and serve the Lord with a greater awareness of my need for the power and direction of the Holy Spirit.

It had been four years since I was last able to attend and the conference has developed in a tremendous way over the past years. It was good before, but it was great this year!

Thank you also for your kindness to allow me to share the time of fellowship after the evening services. Your kindness was and is greatly appreciated.

I thank God for what He is doing through your ministry and through West Coast Baptist College. Thank you for the impact the college is making on our young people.

I look forward to seeing you in December at BIMI. You were missed at the June meeting, but I am glad you were able to have some time with your family.

If I can ever be a blessing or help in any way, please do not hesitate to call.

For the Harvest,

*Bob Wall*

Robert Wall
Pastor

# TBC
## TEMPLE BAPTIST CHURCH

2501 NORTH SHORE BLVD.   FLOWER MOUND, TEXAS 75028   (972) 221-4664   WWW.TEMPLEBC.ORG

October 10, 2003

Dr. Paul Chappell
Lancaster Baptist Church
Lancaster, CA 93535

Dear Dr. Chappell:

I want to thank you and your church for the beautiful flowers for our new auditorium. They added so much to the beauty of the sanctuary.

After having gone through this building program, I marvel that you can be in the building process and still have other buildings on the drawing board. I will pray for the success of all those building programs.

I pray for you often and for your church and its ministries. May God use the young men and women who are being trained in your Bible college, to reach people all over the world with God's wonderful message of salvation.

Thank you again for the wonderful reminder that you were sharing in our joy over being in our new building.

Sincerely,

Richard L. Wallace, Sr.
Pastor

mac

RICHARD L. WALLACE, SR.
PASTOR

25 Years of Ministry          1984 - 2009

# Valley Forge Baptist Temple

"All to the Glory of God." I Cor. 10:31

616 S.Trappe Rd.(Rt. 113)
Collegeville, PA  19426
Phone: (610)948-8100

Scott Wendal
Senior Pastor

Sam Aylestock
Associate Pastor

Lamar Eifert
Associate Pastor

Ron Coulton
Associate Pastor

Greg Joyner
Associate Pastor

Ernie Grooney
Associate Pastor

July 26, 2010

Pastor Paul Chappell
Lancaster Baptist Church
4020 E. Lancaster Blvd.
Lancaster, CA 93535

Dear Pastor Chappell,

WOW!  What a tremendous Spiritual Leadership Conference.  I was truly honored and blessed to be a part of this year's conference.  Jodie and I are delighted to be back next year for the special 25th Anniversary Celebration in 2011.

I want to thank you for once again rolling out the red carpet for Jodie, Megan, and myself.  We want to thank you for the gift bags, the books, the meals, the love offering, but most of all your friendship.

We praise the Lord for the kindred spirit we share.  Thank you for how you take care of our students at WCBC.  We have a young man, Nathan Gifford, that is an incoming freshman from our church studying for the ministry.

Our staff is benefiting greatly from our time there.  They are recharged to do the work of the ministry and lead others to Christ.  This week alone, the Lord has opened the door for me to lead two ladies and a teen to the Lord.  Being soul conscious is synonymous with LBC!!!  All glory to God!

Delighted to Serve,

*Scott Wendal*

Scott Wendal
Sr. Pastor
Valley Forge Baptist Temple

Website:  www.vfbt.org          "The Caring Church"          Email: vfbt@vfbt.com

# TABERNACLE BAPTIST CHURCH
## 115 WEST ELEVENTH ST. - POB 518 - 505 622-7912
## ROSWELL, NEW MEXICO 88202
### *ONSY WHICKER, PASTOR*

*February 19, 1999*

*Dear Brother Chappell,*

*Just a note to thank you for having me speak at the college. I had a wonderful time with the students. It is my prayer that they will go forth and do great and mighty things for God.*

*I would also like to thank you for taking time from your busy schedule to show me the plan and progress on your expansion program. I do pray that you will be ready for the dedication on the 21st of March.*

*Your message Sunday evening blessed my heart. My grand-daughter, Sara, commented on the way home about the good service.*

*Your Friend,*

*Onsy Whicker*

**First Baptist Church**
of LONG BEACH

*Est. 1894*

February 21, 2003

Dr. Paul Chappell
Lancaster Baptist Church
4020 E. Lancaster Blvd.
Lancaster, CA 93535

Dear Dr. Chappell,

Thank you for the delicious meal and sweet fellowship shared at your expense on Tuesday. It will be a treasured memory upon which Linda and I will reflect.

God is so gracious to give to us the blessing of friendship. Your choice to befriend us is humbling and demonstrates the heart for God you have. We have been helped by your advice and encouraged by your kindness.

I often pray for you and glean strength from what God is doing in and through you. Please accept our appreciation and don't hesitate to call on us if we can be of help.

Gratefully Yours,

John Wilkerson
Pastor

# FIRST BAPTIST CHURCH
## of LONG BEACH

**Est. 1894**

March 12, 2004

Dr. Paul Chappell
Lancaster Baptist Church
4020 E. Lancaster Blvd.
Lancaster, CA 93535

Dear Pastor Chappell,

Thanks for the sessions on Monday and Tuesday there in Moreno Valley. They help me and strengthened my vision and practice. God is using you. (Gal. 6:9) Thanks for allowing Him to do so.

I am praying with you regarding the possible acquisition of the school for the LBC ministry. Thanks for being a man of God and a model of Him to others.

Gratefully Yours,

Bro. *PS. 143:10*

John Wilkerson
Pastor

*Thanks for the ideas regarding the auditorium.*

**From the Desk of
Pastor John Wilkerson**

12/3/08

*"...I have made thee a watchman..." Ezekiel 3:17*

Dear Pastor & Mrs. Chappell,

Linda & I have been continually blessed by your kind friendship. Never w/o God's grace could ones do what you have done for us financially, emotionally, physically, and spiritually. Thanks so much!

*First Baptist Church ~ 1000 Pine Ave. ~ Long Beach, CA 90813
(562) 432-8447 ~ www.fbclb.org ~ pastor@fbclb.org*

Bro. John

Ps 143:10

Dear Dr. + Mrs. Chappell,                    1/28/09

Again I find myself + Linda
with reason to express appreciation
for your kindness. The tribute
to Tyler at the WC tourney
was a refreshing event and
another source of comfort. God
has been so very good to us.
We love you and feel
spoiled by God to have you
as friends.

The LBC family + WCBC students
are always so gracious to greet
us and make us feel welcome.

Thanks for making Warwick,
Preston, + Drew feel so special.

Ron Tob
PS. 116:12

John Wilkerson

# From the Desk of
# Pastor John Wilkerson

*"...I have made thee a watchman..." Ezekiel 3:17*

August 6, 2010

Dear Pastor Chappell,

   This is just a brief note to thank you for the continued love and attention given to our family. Thanks for allowing us to speak as a guest in your "Triumphant Living Series".

   The LBC family is a model of grace and receptivity. The time together with you before and after the service was so kind. The meal, treats, gift basket, love offering, fellowship and the room to freshen-up in were also extraordinary.

   We love you and pray regularly for your ministry to expend.

Gratefully Yours,

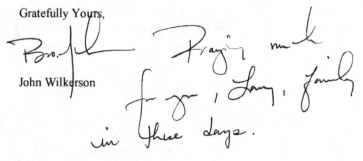

John Wilkerson

*First Baptist Church ~ 1000 Pine Ave. ~ Long Beach, CA 90813*
*(562) 432-8447 ~ www.fbclb.org ~ pastor@fbclb.org*

Rancho Cucamonga, CA                    Pastor Adam G. Zamora

Dear Pastor Chappell,

Wow!  Praise God!!!  Words cannot describe our appreciation to you and the people of Lancaster Baptist.  I am
still in a partial shock, because of the graciousness of you
and your people.  What you did for us was an incredible
encouragement.  My wife and I will have shouting fits for
many days to come.  We are so thankful to you and everyone
at your church.

God makes no mistakes, and I am convinced now more than
ever that God had a divine appointment in us meeting you.
You have been a tremendous blessing to us, not just financially,
but spiritually as well.  Your sermons, counsel, and your
gracious spirit are just phenomenol.  Again, I want you to know
that I am a debtor.  You and your church will have a part in
every changed life at the Mountain View Baptist Church.  I am
so thankful to God for you all.  If you need us to do anything
for you, please let us know.  Wow!!!

                              Sincerely,



                              Adam and Elizabeth Zamora

P.S. We really appreciate the prayers from you all for our baby!


*"The Church That Cares About You"*

*A Church You Can Call "Home!"*

April 3, 2002

Pastor Paul Chappell
4020 E. Lancaster Dr.
Lancaster, CA 93535

Dear Pastor Chappell,

Wow! Praise the Lord for the victory He gave you at your By Faith Night. When I heard all that God did I rejoiced with you. I get excited every time I come to LBC to see all the things God is doing through you all. Thank you for inviting me to be a part of such a night.

God spoke to my heart personally through the preaching of Bro. Gibbs. I will forever look at Barnabas in a different light. In fact, if I could get a copy of that tape I would sure be grateful.

Thank you for your investment in the Mountain View Baptist Church. We will be moving into a new sanctuary Lord-willing on June the 2nd. We are doing a tenant improvement on two suites that recently came available in our business complex. It will allow us to have a sanctuary that will seat 200 and all the classroom space we need. The greatest blessing is that we will meet in one place for all the services. Please pray for us, this is the third time we will go through the C.U.P. process.

Thanks again for allowing me to come to your meeting. I was truly blessed. Have a great day!

Sincerely In Christ,

Adam G. Zamora

*P.O. Box 837, Rancho Cucamonga, California 91729*
*909/484-7002 Pastor Adam Zamora*

# MISSIONARIES
# & FRIENDS FROM
# AROUND THE WORLD

# Mount Hebron

Mount Hebron Baptist Church · Mount Hebron Bible Baptist Institute

Tommy Ashcraft, Pastor · Director

October 18, 2005

Pastor Paul Chappell
Lancaster Baptist Church
4020 E. Lancaster Blvd.
Lancaster, California 93535

Dear Brother Chappell,

Where do I begin to thank you for all the things you and your people did for me last week? Thank you for the comfortable room. Thank you for the snacks and fruit. Thank you for the books. Thank you for the delicious meals, especially on Monday evening at the Ferrso's.

Thank you for allowing me to speak to your people. I was humbled and honored to be in your pulpit both in the Monday evening service, and then again on Tuesday morning for the College chapel service. I understand how a pastor guards his pulpit, and there is no greater honor you could bestow.

Thank you for allowing me to spend time with your wonderful College students. They are a promising group of young people. Some of them are children of people I have known for years. I am glad there is a West Coast Baptist College they can attend.

Thank you for the generous love offering. Most of all, thank you for your genuine friendship. I have respected and admired you for many years, and I count it one a great privileges to consider you my friend.

I don't know if I have ever been so impressed by a ministry as I was by Lancaster Baptist Church. There is a sense of healthiness and balance that is rare in any ministry, and especially one comprised of as many young Christians as yours has.

May God's best continue to be yours. We will be praying about the projects you have for this year. Please pray for us as we continue to do our best in reaching souls as your representatives.

Your friend and servant,

Tommy Ashcraft

---

**Tommy Ashcraft is an independent Baptist missionary sent by First Baptist Church, Hammond, IN, Dr. Jack Schaap, Pastor**
**Field Address:** Dr. Tommy Ashcraft  Apartado 2592  Monterrey, N. L. Mexico  **Telephone:** 011 52 (818) 266-1356
**Support Address:** Mount Hebron  P. O. Box 1149  McAllen, TX 78505  **Email:** tommyashcraft@prodigy.net.mx

# BIBLE BAPTIST CHURCH

신학박사
담임목사  김 우 생
서울특별시 은평구 불광동 242 – 3
불광동성서침례교회

Dr. Daniel Wooseang Kim. Pastor
242-3, Bul Kwang Dong,
Eun Pyeng Gu, Seoul, 122-041 Korea
Tel: 359-0559, 355-7887 Fax: 358-0110

July 26, 2000


Dr. Paul Chappell
Lancaster Baptist Church
4020 E. Lancaster Blvd.
Lancaster, CA 93535


Dear Dr. Chappell,

Greetings in the wonderful Name of our Lord Jesus Christ from Seoul, Korea.

I came back to Seoul from Lancaster, with the experience of excitement and inspiration. It was one of the highlights of my 40 years of ministry for the Lord. Thank you for your hospitality and thoughtfulness in everyway while we were there. Your staff and people are exceptionally kind, dedicated, and inspirational. You all were such a blessing to us. I believe with all my heart that Lancaster Baptist Church is a model church for all Independent Baptist Churches in this century.

Especially, I appreciate that on the very first night of the Spiritual Leadership Conference, you honored me by giving me the Servant Leadership Award, although I don't think I deserve to receive it. And even though it was a small part, I was glad that I could participate in the building project for Lori Thompson Dormitory.

And let us not be weary in well doing: for in due season we shall reap, if we faint not.   Galatian 6:9

# BIBLE BAPTIST CHURCH

신학박사
담임목사  김 우 생
서울특별시 은평구 불광동 242 – 3
불광동성서침례교회

Dr. Daniel Wooseang Kim. Pastor
242-3, Bul Kwang Dong,
Eun Pyeng Gu, Seoul, 122-041 Korea
Tel :359-0559, 355-7887 Fax :358-0110

Thank you again for your generous love offering, and for taking care of us – with wonderful meals and nice cars.

We are looking forward to hosting the Spiritual Leadership Conference Asia in November 12 through 15, and to having you and others who will participate in the Conference.

We love you.

Because of Calvary's love,

Daniel Kim

---

And let us not be weary in well doing: for in due season we shall reap, if we faint not.   Galatian 6:9

# BIBLE BAPTIST CHURCH

신학박사
담임목사  김 우 생
서울특별시 은평구 불광동 242-3
불광동성서침례교회

Dr. Daniel Wooseang Kim. Pastor
242-3, Bul Kwang Dong,
Eun Pyeng Gu, Seoul, 122-041 Korea
Tel: 359-0559, 355-7887 Fax: 358-0110

December 7, 2000

Dr. Paul Chappell
Lancaster Baptist Church
4020 E. Lancaster Blvd.
Lancaster, CA 93535

Dear Dr. Chappell,

Greetings from BulKwangDong Bible Baptist Church!

I want to write to you and tell you that we had numerous comments about the Spiritual Leadership Conference Asia since you left Seoul. We had letters, e-mails and phone calls from pastors, saying that this Conference was a great blessing and a challenge to them, especially on soul winning. Many of them said that it was a turning point in their ministry, and that they are starting anew with a clear vision and a focus on winning souls for Christ. They also pointed out that this Conference was offered for the pastors in Korea at the most appropriate time.

I am more than sure that God had greatly used this Conference to challenge and to encourage Korean pastors and missionaries from Asian countries. I know all this was possible because you and the other speakers came and delivered God's precious truths to us. I appreciate you so much for coming and for being such a blessing to all of us.

I also thank you for inviting me to the Spiritual Leadership Conference 2002, in Lancaster. I am looking forward to being with you, and to another great time.

And let us not be weary in well doing: for in due season we shall reap, if we faint not.    Galatian 6:9

# BIBLE BAPTIST CHURCH

신학박사
담임목사  김  우  생
서울특별시 은평구 불광동 242 – 3
불광동성서침례교회

Dr. Daniel Wooseang Kim. Pastor
242-3, Bul Kwang Dong,
Eun Pyeng Gu, Seoul, 122-041 Korea
Tel : 359-0559, 355-7887 Fax : 358-0110

Thank you, and we love you.

Because of Calvary's love,

Daniel Wooseang Kim

---

And let us not be weary in well doing : for in due season we shall reap, if we faint not.   Galatian 6 : 9

# BIBLE BAPTIST CHURCH

### Dr. Daniel Wooseang Kim. Pastor

### http://www.bkdbbc.org

242-3, Bul Kwang Dong, Eun Pyeng Gu, Seoul, 122-856 Korea
Tel:82-2-359-0559,355-7887  Fax:82-2-358-0110
E-mail : bbchurch@chollian.net
kim38110@chollian.net

2006-07-26

Dr. Paul Chappell
Lancaster Baptist Church
4020 E. Lancaster Blvd.
Lancaster, CA 93535

Dear Bro. Chappell,

We came back with hearts full of excitement and inspiration from being in Lancaster Baptist Church's 20th Anniversary and the Spiritual Leadership Conference.  I can only say that it was amazing and marvelous to see God using you to do such a great job.  I praise God for you and your leadership!

Especially your message on faith through Christ and striving together for the Gospel of Christ was really a blessing to me.  It touched my heart and made me rededicate myself for the ministry of reaching souls and for doing the great work that God has committed to me.

Thank you for your love and friendship toward us and also for the generous hospitality you've shown us.  We truly appreciate it so much.  Also, we thank your staff and your people for their kindness.  They certainly showed servant leadership, which means they were trained by a great servant leader.

Those pastors who went with me this time told me how they were inspired by being in your church.  They said your church is a model church and that they would like to be in a church like yours.  I'm sure the impression would be inscribed in their hearts.

And let us not be weary in well doing: for in due season we shall reap, if we faint not.  Galatians 6:9

# BIBLE BAPTIST CHURCH

### Dr. Daniel Wooseang Kim. Pastor

### http://www.bkdbbc.org

242-3, Bul Kwang Dong, Eun Pyeng Gu, Seoul, 122-856 Korea
Tel:82-2-359-0559,355-7887   Fax:82-2-358-0110
E-mail : bbchurch@chollian.net
kim38110@chollian.net

Thank you again for the opportunity to participate in 20th Anniversary and the Spiritual Leadership Conference of your church.   Thank you for your friendship. We love you dearly.   May God continue to bless you!

Because of Calvary's love,

Daniel Wooseang Kim
Senior Pastor
BulKwangDong Bible Baptist Church
Seoul, Korea

---

And let us not be weary in well doing: for in due season we shall reap, if we faint not.   Galatians 6:9

**THE MARTINS**
Your Missionaries in the Philippines

December 25, 2007

Dear Brother Chappell,

It's Christmas day here, and I was thinking of the Lord today and His goodness to me. I was also thinking about you and your friendship and how that has affected me and the work the Lord has given us to do here. I wanted to thank you for, not only the things you have done for me, but for your example as a leader and as a Christian. I pray for you each day as I do not know how you handle all the difficulties you encounter and pressure you must feel. I know it is very hard to pastor a church in the U.S. I often thank God that He did not call me to do that. Of course, the ministry God has given you involves a load that very few pastors will ever have or understand. I also wanted to tell you how much I respect you for keeping on and being faithful to Him year after year.

I want to thank you specifically for some things. First I want to thank you for coming to visit us this year. It was one of the highlights of my life to have you here during one of our Pastors and Workers Conferences. I also want to thank you for helping us with the project of the music CD. Brother Schmidt has been keeping us updated, and I don't know how to begin to thank you. I don't know what we would have done without your help. Thank you for sending two of your best, Clark and Rachel, to this country as missionaries. They are such good representatives of your ministry. It seems like all the people you have sent here on the mission trips have been great in their attitude and service. Lastly, I want to thank you for the way you have raised your children. I'm sure you must be so proud of them. I am too. I only wish I could have known your kids for a lot longer than I have.

I'm sorry for writing such a long note. I just wanted to let you know that on the day people rejoice in the arrival of our Great Saviour, that many (including myself) are grateful that he sent someone like you to be such a blessing to our lives.

God bless,

Rick Martin

**FIELD ADDRESS:**
P.O Box 88, Iloilo City, Philippines 5000
Tel # (63-33) 3204557
Fax # (63-33) 3203677

**MISSION ADDRESS:**
Baptist International Missions, Inc.
Box 9215, Chattanooga, Tn 37412

**HOME ADDRESS:**
1899 Saddleback Blvd., #4
Norman OK 73072, USA
405-329-8515

Baptist Church
3-11-32 Imamiya
Mino-city Osaka 562-0033 Japan
Phone:072.726.0726
Fax:072.726.0276
E-mail office@senrinewtown.com
URL http://www.senrinewtown.com

July 16, 2007

Dr. Paul Chappell
Lancaster Baptist Church
4020 E. Lancaster Blvd.
Lancaster, CA 93535
U.S.A.


Dear Dr. Paul Chappell,

Thank you so much for your kindness and hospitality for the Spiritual Leadership
Conference in spite of your busy schedule.

I am truly thankful to God for me to attend this year's conference. God has given me many
blessings, fruitful lessons, abundant grace, great challenges and visions.

Please continue to pray for churches and souls in Japan.
I remember you and your ministry in prayers.


With gratitude,

Eriya Ogawa
Senri Newtown Baptist Church

SENRI NEWTOWN

**Senri Newtown**
**Baptist Church**
3-11-32 Imamiya
Mino-city Osaka 562-0033 Japan
Phone:072.726.0726
Fax:072.726.0276
E-mail office@senrinewtown.com
URL http://www.senrinewtown.com

June 12, 2010

Dear Dr. Paul Chappell.

Greetings in His Name

Praise the Lord for His many blessings upon you and your church
I am grateful for you to give me a chance to have a session in
the Leaders Conference . I am a poor Japanese pastor. But
Please pray for me to be used of God in the Conference.
By the way. I received a check of $1,100 for my air fare
yesterday. I was surprised with your kindness.
Thank you so very much . I know that you are so busy
for the Conference I want you to know that I am praying
for your preparation for the Conference I will come to
Lancaster on July 10. with my wife Dr. Don Sisk knows my arrival time.
I am looking forward to seeing you
Thank you so much for your prayers and kindness

In Him

Sogoro Ogawa.

**SENRI NEWTOWN**
**BAPTIST CHURCH**

*Serving our Generation ... Reaching the Next*

*Dr. James Ray*
President & General Director

October 13, 2008

Dr. Paul W. Chappell
Lancaster Baptist Church
4020 E. Lancaster Blvd.
Lancaster, CA 93535

Dear Dr. Chappell:

I was not able to get to you during the Nationwide Baptist Fellowship, but I wanted to tell you how much Mary and I both were challenged by your great message. Thank you for mentioning the new book and also for recognizing BIMI during your introduction. That, of course, was so much appreciated.

Dr. Chappell, we continue to stand in awe at what God is doing through you and your wife and through that great ministry at Lancaster. Please be assured of our continued prayers for you in every way. Thank you also for serving us as a Trustee of Baptist International Missions. Your participation and fellowship in that great work is always such an encouragement.

I remain…

Your friend for the harvest,

James R. Ray
President, BIMI

JRR:ljb

**BAPTIST INTERNATIONAL MISSIONS, INC.**

Australia

Dear Dr Chappell                                                    12 September, 2006

I wanted to take a moment to express to you my deep appreciation for the kindness and hospitality you showed toward me while I was in Lancaster for the Spiritual Leadership Conference.

You were very kind to me in so many ways. I had a beautiful hotel room, I think even better than most of the other speakers. The gift basket was large and filled with wonderful things and the ladies who delivered it were very kind and courteous. I felt I was being honoured much more than I deserved. I wondered if I accidentally got Dr Gibbs room and basket ☺

On top of all this you went out of your way to include me in events I was not worthy to attend. The dinners at the church and Sunday lunch in your home, I was amazed at your energy and thoughtfulness throughout my entire visit. Preacher I say this most sincerely, I was very impressed with your gracious spirit, It was to me moving and very Christ like. I went away thinking how deserving you are of the successes you have enjoyed. I am sure you will be immediately thinking that Christ alone has made it all possible and I agree, but allow me to also express recognition and honour to the servant that Christ has used. I am so happy in my heart for you. I feel compelled to pray for you and ask God to give you more and to sustain you with His grace for all that you must bare.

I feel that Lancaster Baptist Church has no limits for its future. I see some men seek for success for what it offers them but I believe with you, this is not so. I have watched you and listened carefully when you preach and talk and it seems to me your motives for wanting growth are right. You sincerely seek souls for Christ and you want God to have the Glory from all that happens at Lancaster Baptist. It is this right motive that positions you for continued blessings.

You are the right person to exercise influence and leadership over America's Independent Baptist Churches because you are a man of Grace and balance. I see how you urge other Pastors to take the higher road and when you rebuke you do it with mercy and sometimes humor. I am thrilled to be watching something happen at Lancaster that future generations will talk of. I am so privileged to have been offered your friendship.

www.baptist.com.au

P +617 3264 3476
F +617 3264 5189

Australia

Preacher, may I say also how impressed I was with your family. I watched them serve when I had dinner at your home and I was moved to tears as I saw them speak of how God has used you, their dad, through these years. It is obvious they love you deeply and respect you not only as their father but a true man of God. A mans ways are known by his own family more than any other and to see the way they felt about you confirmed my judgment of your character and person as being correct. I am so happy for you that you have the family you have.

Thank you Preacher for the suit you purchased for me, for use of a car, and for the opportunity to be there to celebrate a great moment in the life of Lancaster Baptist Church. I learned some things from the preaching and teaching which I hope I can remember and apply. I learned even more from quietly observing your manner and way of life. I look forward to a continued friendship and trust that all will be ok for your coming to Australia in June 2008.

Yours sincerely, yours in friendship…

Wayne Sehmish

www.baptist.com.au

P +617 3264 3476
F +617 3264 5189

# OTHER SERVANTS OF GOD

# Pacific Coast Baptist Bible College

1100 SOUTH VALLEY CENTER • SAN DIMAS, CALIFORNIA 91773 • PHONE (714) 599-6843

June 27, 1978

**PRESIDENT**
TED HICKS, TH.D.
**VICE-PRESIDENT**
JOHN W. WILLIAMS, JR.
**EXEC. VICE-PRESIDENT**
JACK BASKIN, D.D.
**ADMIN. ASSISTANT**
WAYNE JAMES, PH.D.
**SECRETARY**
JOSEPH MORTON
**TRUSTEES**
KEN ADRIAN
TOM BRIDGES
GEORGE GOLDEN
J. C. JOINER
JOE PENROD
JERRY PREVO
HOMER QUINLAN
THOMAS RAY
BILL WHITAKER

**WESTERN STATES
BAPTIST BIBLE FELLOWSHIP**

**PRESIDENT**
LLOYD LEDBETTER
**VICE PRESIDENT**
D. W. ARNELL
**SECRETARY**
GARY WILSON
**TREASURER**
DUANE PETTIPIECE

Paul Chappell
Suh Dah Moon Ku
Box 44
Seoul, KOREA  120

Dear Paul:

I sure was glad we got to spend some time talking and praying.  I have confidence that you are going to begin the ministry we talked about.  Please let me know how it works.

Please use the application and plan to come in January.

Please remember a strong will is great when it is completely yielded to God.

Your friend,

Brother Jack

JB:bf
Enc.

*Co-workers with the Baptist
Bible Fellowship International*

# Pacific Coast Baptist Bible College

1100 SOUTH VALLEY CENTER • SAN DIMAS, CALIFORNIA 91773 • PHONE (714) 599-6843

**PRESIDENT**
TED HICKS, TH.D.
**VICE-PRESIDENT**
JOHN W. WILLIAMS, JR.
**EXEC. VICE-PRESIDENT**
JACK BASKIN, D.D.
**ADMIN. ASSISTANT**
WAYNE JAMES, PH.D.
**SECRETARY**
JOSEPH MORTON
**TRUSTEES**
KEN ADRIAN
TOM BRIDGES
GEORGE GOLDEN
J. C. JOINER
JOE PENROD
JERRY PREVO
HOMER QUINLAN
THOMAS RAY
BILL WHITAKER

**WESTERN STATES
BAPTIST BIBLE FELLOWSHIP**

**PRESIDENT**
LLOYD LEDBETTER
**VICE PRESIDENT**
D. W. ARNELL
**SECRETARY**
GARY WILSON
**TREASURER**
DUANE PETTIPIECE

September 13, 1978

Paul Chappell
Baptist Oriental Missions
P. O. Box 85
Pomona, CA 91769

Dear Paul:

I was so thrilled to hear from you and learn
how God is using you. I am glad to know that you
are a man of your word. You will recall you assured
me you would be getting involved as we had prayer
together near the chapel.

Please give my love to all your family. I shall
look forward to seeing you.

Yours and His,

Jack Baskin

Jack Baskin

JB:bf
Enc.

*Co-workers with the Baptist
Bible Fellowship International*

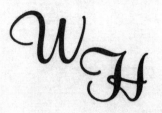

Western Hills Baptist Church
Dr. Jack Baskin, Pastor
Rev. Steve Baskin, Co-pastor

January 30, 1995

Dr. Paul Chappell
Lancaster Baptist Church
304 W. Lancaster Blvd.
Lancaster, CA 93534

Dear Bro. Paul,

Your sermon in the January 27 issue of the Sword of the Lord was simply profound. Both of the last two words describe it. It was profound in that you really exalted the eternal Son of God. It was simple in that even a child should be able to understand it.

I was and am very proud of you.

Sincerely,

Bro. Jack Baskin

JB/mj

700 Mars Hill Road, Kennesaw, Georgia 30144 • Phone (404) 425-7118

**SEOUL PLAZA HOTEL**

Brother Paul:                    Feb 15, 1989

You have been a real joy to be with on this trip. I was truly blessed by the opportunity to be with you!

God's hand is on you Paul. I am more dededicated to pray for you asking God for the very best for you and your dear family. Thank you for your friendship.

Dave — David. C. Gibbs, Jr.

#23, 2-KA, TAIPYUNG-RO, CHUNG-KU, SEOUL, KOREA TEL: (02) 771-22, TELEX: K26215, K24424 FAX: (02) 756-3610 CABLE: PLAZAHL SEOUL

# GIBBS & CRAZE

*Attorneys and Counselors at Law*

| OHIO OFFICE: | FLORIDA OFFICE: | CALIFORNIA OFFICE: |
|---|---|---|
| **GIBBS & CRAZE CO., L.P.A.** | **GIBBS & CRAZE, P. A.** | **GIBBS & CRAZE** |
| 7055 ENGLE ROAD, SUITE 502 | 5666 SEMINOLE BOULEVARD, SUITE TWO | 1550 EL CAMINO REAL, SUITE 220 |
| CLEVELAND, OHIO 44130 | SEMINOLE, FLORIDA 33772 | MENLO PARK, CALIFORNIA 94025 |

TELEPHONE: (813) 399-8300

FAX: (813) 398-3907

**PLEASE RESPOND TO:**
Florida Office

November 21, 1996

Pastor Paul Chappell
Lancaster Baptist Church
4020 East Lancaster Boulevard
Lancaster, CA 93535

Dear Pastor Chappell:

When a man is greatly used of God, his life always comes to those moments where some very critical reassessments have to be made. It is how we respond to these periods of reevaluation that can indeed make all of the difference in the world as to how the Lord leads in the waiting periods of our lives.

These seasons of measurement are brought on by the loving ministry of the Holy Spirit who is endeavoring to get us to make the periodic midcourse changes that are so vital to the successful completion of our course. The tool of emotion, which the Holy Spirit often uses during these times, is a feeling of a need for reassurance in our spirit, or a sense of detached dissatisfaction. This is done to capture our attention and to prepare us for the needed change. The man who surprisingly "works through" these periods when the Holy Spirit is endeavoring to get him to change is engaged in a perilous pursuit. He is placing in position in the course of his life the signpost which reads, "I will not change" and "I will not yield." In time, the Holy Spirit will withdraw His prompting from this man. He will proceed with his ministry exactly as he was before, feeling quite sure that what he experienced was nothing more than a simple emotional upset or, at worst, some notice of a humanly manufactured midlife or career crisis. But having "weathered it" and "gotten over it," he is ready to go on for the Lord, little realizing the frustration to the leading of God he has brought about in his life.

There are moments in the life of every Christian when through fatigue, illness or other frustrating circumstances we can feel a sense of despair or an element of dissatisfaction. But that is normally distinguishably different from when the Spirit of God moves with His prompting to prepare us for even greater usefulness for the cause of Christ. When the emotions we are experiencing are due to fatigue and matters of that nature, there is almost always a recognition certain within our hearts of what the problem is and what we can do to correct it.

# GIBBS & CRAZE
*Attorneys and Counselors at Law*

Pastor Paul Chappell
November 21, 1996
Page 2

But when the Holy Spirit is moving upon us to disquiet our emotions and spirit for the reason of causing a change in our lives, we find ourselves more often baffled as to why we would feel the way that we are. Our reasoning says, "How, when the Lord is so blessing and perpetuating what we are venturing for Him, could feel as I do?" In fact, we feel as sense of guilt at times as to how we could feel like this amidst all that the Lord is accomplishing.

The key in these moments of life is to seize upon all that the Lord is causing us to experience. We must not grieve or defeat the work of God's leading, but we should recognize the discomfort in our hearts as His schooling in us. To simply wait out His pull upon our heart is a tragedy recorded repeatedly in Scripture; however, when our spirit responds to the impulse of His leading, God is able to use us in greater measure.

Some would teach and preach that we are not to feel these moments of disquiet within our spirit (as they say that they never do), but I do not feel that to be the position of the Scriptures. David, so greatly used of God, bares his emotions and state of mind in the Psalms for all to read. The Bible is our almost continuous record of men and women whom the Lord used and changed when they stayed sensitive to His moving upon their spirit and emotion.

I have said all of this, Pastor, because after our time of fellowship and sharing together, I believe that the Lord is striving to effectuate a change in both of our lives. The Lord has so greatly used and blessed the efforts of you and your dear wife! I have absolutely no doubt as to the fact that your ministry is in its imperative infancy in regard to all that the Lord is going to use the two of you to accomplish. I personally believe that the Lord has chosen you and Mrs. Chappell to raise a voice and presence for Him which is going to be heard effectively not only across Southern California, but across the entire nation and around the world! I am excited for you and Mrs. Chappell beyond my ability to be able to express it because of what God has done, is doing, and is going to do in your lives. You are two of the dearest people that I know. I treasure your friendship as a wonderful gift from the Lord.

Greatness for God requires greatness with God. And that is where the acute sensitivity and right reading of what the Lord is leading us to when He begins these moments of uneasiness in our hearts, are so vital. These seasons in our spirit are no accident of oversight with God. Rather, they are His mid-course graduate school for great usefulness.

You and you alone, Pastor, have to discern what the Lord is saying in these attentive, capturing moments with Him. Each message from God to His servant is virtually personal. And I would always be cautious when someone else endeavors to bring upon you his understanding of what the Lord wants in your life or ministry. For, outside of the Lord's expressed will in His Word, the Lord's leading and message to each is not for another to interpret or redirect.

So I am offering all that I am saying with a very reserved deference and honor to you, Pastor. I bid you to be a great Christian, a great pastor and preacher, and a loving and exemplary husband and father. But with all of the demands being made upon your time I feel

# GIBBS & CRAZE
*Attorneys and Counselors at Law*

Pastor Paul Chappell
November 21, 1996
Page 3

that it is possible that the Lord is raising a moment of disquiet in your heart because the ever-expanding role the ministry is playing is totally capturing your time. Because your ministry is so worthy and of such honor to the Lord, we can easily justify giving it all of our time and priority of attention. But the man of God has to guard his own walk with the Lord and his time with his family above this. He has to capture his schedule before his schedule captures him.

I would offer the following suggestions for your consideration, Preacher, but if you don't feel led to do any of them, it will only be because you have sensed the Lord leading in a better way.

(1)     Schedule weekly to get away so that you can spend some truly intimate time with the Lord. Get to a place where you can separate yourself from the pressure of what will come up that day so that you can relax and truly have "time" with the Lord. Nothing is more important for your church or family than that you have taken the time to do this. With the schedule you are keeping, time for an intimacy with the Lord will never just make itself available. You will have to put it in the schedule and defend its existence with the same fervor that you would a promised preaching engagement. This time with God will be your making! And the failure to keep these appointments with God will begin to undermine every effort that we make for Him.

Set it! Keep it! And, above all, thoroughly love and enjoy your time with the Master! Don't be fooled into thinking that laboring for Him is the same as being with Him. Put His time first, which is where it belongs.

(2)     Schedule your family with time that carries a greater priority than everything else, save your time with the Lord. Because our families are gracious and love us so much, they never make demands which cast themselves upon our schedules. So what does make demands goes on our calendars first, and our families get what is left—that is, if there is any time left. This goes on until we feel so guilty about it to continue that we cancel some things to make some room for the family for a few hours, days, or weeks. But shortly the schedule will fill in again and our family has to wait (which they will graciously do) until we at some time in the future squeeze them in again.

There is no question that we love our families more than we could ever say, but we need to be sure that our schedules consistently reflect that love. Because our schedules control our lives, it is imperative that our commitments of love control our schedule. Your time of impact upon your dear children's lives is racing by. The pastorate is full of good men who wanted to spend time in the lives of their family after their family had already created lives with little of their involvement. Our future with our family is forged in the schedule we make them a part of today. Schedule your time with the Lord and your family first. Schedule it as certain as you would the highlight of your church activity calendar. Set it certain, and defend it faithfully. The devil knows how critical your time with the Lord and your family is. It is his plan to attach with important activity these critical activities with the hope that you will let the important crowd out the critical from life and schedule.

# GIBBS & CRAZE
*Attorneys and Counselors at Law*

Pastor Paul Chappell
November 21, 1996
Page 4

Remember, if you give one hundred percent of your time to the ministry at the total exclusion of any time with the Lord or your family, it won't be enough. If God gives you days which are forty-eight hours in length, it still won't be enough time. Your ministry will always cry out with increasing magnitude for more of you. It will cry out for more than you can humanly give.

The key is not giving it more time, but having God's divine anointing upon each moment that is indeed given. Save the Lord makes each moment count beyond its actual increment of time, your life's effectiveness is limited by the time available. But, with your schedule honoring what the Lord put first—your time with Him and your family—He will enable your efforts beyond your means of actual time.

There are some good men who need to have a fire built under them when it comes to working harder. (You certainly are not in that category.) But working hard at the expense of not giving the Lord and one's family a scheduled priority can be disastrous in consequence as not working hard at all. The key for any pastor is that he learns to control his schedule, disallowing his schedule to control him.

Please pray for me as I am working on this in my own life and ministry. I love you and your dear family. Thank you for being my friend.

Sincerely in Christ,

*David C. Gibbs, Jr.*

David C. Gibbs, Jr.
Admitted in Ohio

DCG/kmg

# CHRISTIAN LAW ASSOCIATION

*A Ministry of Helps to Bible-believing Churches and Christians*

TELEPHONE: (813) 399-8300          POST OFFICE BOX 4010          FAX: (813) 398-3907
                                    SEMINOLE, FLORIDA 33775-4010

August 25, 1998

Pastor Paul Chappell
Lancaster Baptist Church
4020 East Lancaster Boulevard
Lancaster, CA 93535

Dear Pastor Chappell:

Thank you, my friend, for your great kindness in allowing me to have the honor of preaching at your Pastor's Leadership Conference. My heart was truly moved by the messages preached by the other dear men of God, and your preaching and instruction was nothing short of spectacular. By the Lord's gracious enablement, you giftedly combined a Christ-honoring instructional challenge with an encouraging compassion. It is so very rare to see the Lord speak so decisively yet compassionately as He did through you, Brother Chappell. It was truly a remarkable conference!

If the Lord would give you the liberty to do so, and if you would think it wise, please consider making some of your sessions annual presentations. Your sessions in our response to adversity are crucial in the hour in which we live. For any church or ministry which stands faithful to the Word will be assured of an ever-increasing diet of opposition and adverse thunderings; and, as you so ably pointed out in your teaching, our response as well as our stand are equally directed by the Word of God. The right stand which is taken the wrong way is as Biblically disastrous as the wrong stand. Please consider reinforcing this critical instruction each year.

I would also most strongly encourage you to keep representing your material in the Biblically-balanced aspect of your ministry. This I would consider vital beyond my ability to express. As I have the privilege to travel America and see our treasured Independent Fundamental Baptist churches, I am constantly burdened with the fact that they are struggling with the seemingly-insurmountable task of trying to strike a Christ-honoring balance in their labors. The material you gave on this perplexing problem was profound and yet imminently practical. This teaching cannot ever be repeated too often, for what I find is that churches who are almost decisively pushing one aspect of Christian endeavor at the expense of so many other Biblically-commanded considerations are what most often become a course of self-destruction. Your balance as you maintain a ministry which meets the spectrum of Biblical responsibilities is so very, very needed.

We truly love and appreciate you and your dear family, Pastor. In my life I treasure your friendship as a great gift from the Lord. You are a source of great joy to my heart.

The beautiful award which you presented to me was certainly undeserved, but I treasure it more than I can ever begin to say because of the great love with which you gave it to me. I have both cried and joyed over your giving me this exceptionally-beautiful award. Thank you for being so very tender-hearted and kind to me, my family, and our ministry.

Pastor Chappell
August 25, 1998
Page Two

I have already put next year's Leadership Conference on my prayer list. I am asking the Lord to give you even greater insight and divinely-granted power for the challenges which must surely lie ahead. I would be most honored if you would grant me the privilege of praying over any special needs or requests you may be burdened with for next year's conference. Never forget that the only place that power ever comes before prayer is in the dictionary. In life, prayer is always the precedent to God's power. Please let me know what I can pray for that would be a help to you.

Thank you again for your great kindness to me.

Very truly yours,

David C. Gibbs, Jr.

# CHRISTIAN LAW ASSOCIATION

*A Ministry of Helps to Bible-believing Churches and Christians*

TELEPHONE: (727) 399-8300     POST OFFICE BOX 4010     FAX: (727) 398-3907
SEMINOLE, FLORIDA 33775-4010

March 19, 1999

Pastor Paul Chappell
Lancaster Baptist Church
4020 E. Lancaster Blvd.
Lancaster, CA 93535

Dear Pastor Chappell:

Your preaching is always a blessing to my heart and life. But in Tacoma, Washington, I sensed that the Lord moved in and took over in your message in a way that is going to make a telling difference in my life as well as in the lives of all that were there. You preached conviction, challenge, and compassion in that rare Bible balance that makes it so convicting yet irresistibly attractive. God used you, my friend, and there is no higher compliment that can every be given to any man of God or preacher than that.

Your encouragement to Pastor Smith is heaven sent fuel for his soul. He so admires how you are standing for Christ and he has purposed to be attentive to learn everything from you that he possibly can. I am to the very best of my ability, Brother Chappell, trying to encourage Pastor Smith (as well as the other preachers) to learn from you all that they can. It is so important that they not just learn "how to do it", but of far greater importance that they learn "how to be it." And your life is that which I am fervently praying the Lord will continue to use to teach through the most.

I was so very proud of you and Mrs. Chappell. I love you both more than I can ever begin to say. Your friendship is one of the Lord's sweetest blessings to me. Your family, and how you are as a family serving God, is one of my life's greatest pleasures.

Pastor Paul Chappell
March 25, 1999
Page 2

Thank you for your friendship and thank you for loving me, my family, and our ministry. I am praying for the Lord to increase your "tribe" as never before.

Very truly yours,

David C. Gibbs, Jr.

DCG/sc

Dear Brother Chappell,

A year or two ago, when we were at West Coast, you arranged for Brother Schmidt & Dana to take Shelly & me to Club 33 in Disneyland. At the time, you said you didn't know what Club 33 was. I recently came across the enclosed info on Club 33 & thought you might enjoy reading it.

Thank you so much for including us in the Leadership Conference this year. It was a great blessing to me personally. Everything was outstanding. Your focus in ministy is so needed. I will also continue to uphold your family in prayer. They are such a testimony of God's grace.

Rejoicing in the Lord

Phil 4:4

Thank you for all of your gracious gifts.

Dear Brother Chappell,

What a blessing it was for Shelly & me to get to spend some time with you & Terrie, & the rest of your family. How I thank God for your friendship & your ministry. The conference … my, oh my … was fantastic! We were encouraged, challenged, convicted, and blessed beyond words. Thank you also for the Servant / Leadership award — what a shock!

It was so much fun to be with all of you at the Dodgers game. We also thoroughly enjoyed Jon, your son in law. God has blessed us in some unusual ways since our time with you, particularly in the area of soulwinning. Thank you for your faithfulness & your friendship. Rejoicing in the Lord! Ron
Phil. 4:4

# PLEASANT VALLEY BAPTIST CHURCH

July 11, 2002

Pastor Paul Chappell
Lancaster Baptist Church
4020 East Lancaster Blvd.
Lancaster, CA 93535

Dear Pastor Chappell:

Thank you very much for the plant and card for my ordination service. Ministry is even more exciting than I ever dreamed. Please, thank the church and college for all of their investment. Pastor, thank you for all of the time we spent together, I relive those talks often. I want to be like you in so many ways. Please, pray for us that God will use us in a special way here at Pleasant Valley Baptist Church.

If there is ever anything I can do for you, please, do not hesitate to let me know.

Because He Lives,

Gabriel Ruhl
Assistant Pastor

13539 GARNER LANE • CHICO, CA • 95973
PHONE: (530) 343-0555 • FAX: (530) 894-7823

**Evangelist Paul Schwanke**

*Lakeside Baptist Church Evangelism*
*38036 North 15th Avenue*
*Desert Hills, Arizona 85086*
(623) 910-5747
ps@preachthebible.com

June 14, 2008

Pastor Paul Chappell
Lancaster Baptist Church
4020 E Lancaster Blvd
Lancaster, CA 93535

Dear Brother Chappell,

I wanted to write and thank you for the opportunity to preach once again at the men's campout this year. It was a great encouragement for me to see so many men gather with a heart for the Bible. I praise the Lord for their reception to the preaching, and I trust the Lord will bless with fruit in the days ahead from that meeting.

Thanks as well for the generous offering given to us, and for the gracious gift and plaque commemorating the years God has allowed me to preach. I appreciate as well your gracious kindness to my wife Cathy.

We are excited to see how God continues to build His work in Lancaster. Be encouraged in the Lord and keep in the battle.

Looking for the Blessed Hope,

Paul Schwanke

*25 Years of Preaching the Cross ... the Power of God*

# SERVANTS OF GOD
# NOW WITH THE LORD

W. A. CRISWELL, PASTOR EMERITUS
FIRST BAPTIST CHURCH
DALLAS, TEXAS 75201

February 11, 1997

Dr. Paul Chappell, Pastor
Lancaster Baptist Church
4020 East Lancaster Blvd
Lancaster, CA   93535

Dear wonderful pastor, Dr. Paul Chappell:

Your letter of February 3 is absolutely one of the most astonishing I have ever received in all my long life of 87 years and 71 years in the ministry. When I reached my 80's, our church was beginning to go over 8000 in Sunday School attendance. The size of the church in no way and in no wise hindered its many faceted ministries. God blessed it all, up and down and through and through. My experience in this First Baptist Church of Dallas is confirmed by other pastors and leaders in the Mega Churches of our Convention and in like congregations of other faiths.

Absolutely and positively, you pay no attention to those critics. I, personally, have never heard of a criticism like that. You stand true to the faith, preach the Gospel, and ask God to help you reach thousands and thousands of other people who need the Lord.

Faithfully and devotedly,

your fellow pastor,

W. A. Criswell

ep

# A d d i c t i o n   A b s t i n e n c e   P r o g r a m

March 5, 2003

Dr. Paul Chappell
Lancaster Baptist Church
4020 E. Lancaster Blvd.
Lancaster, CA 93535

Dear Dr. Chappell:

Thank you for the opportunity of spending time with you. It was an honor to be apart of your staff meeting, teach your Master's class, and preach in your College Chapel.

I appreciated the attentiveness of the students in the Master's class. It was great to have so many show an interest and ask questions concerning the ministry.

The spirit of the students during chapel was awesome (California word ☺)! Praise the Lord for their tender hearts and response to God's Word. I am thankful for your willingness to provide a place where young people can prepare to serve God and others.

I anticipate hearing of the great things God will do through your ministry and our ministry there. If ever I can be of service to you please don't hesitate to call.

Yours for the addicted,

Steven Curington
President

PO Box 15732 • Loves Park, IL 61132 • tel 815-986-0460
Email: runanimous@aol.com • Web: www.reformu.com

# North Valley Baptist Church
### of Santa Clara, California
### Nine Forty-One Clyde Avenue

June 14, 1990

Pastor Paul Chappell
Lancaster Baptist Church
304 W. Lancaster Blvd.
Lancaster, CA 93534

Dear Brother Chappell,

I wanted to take just a moment to drop you a line to express my gratitude to you for all that you have done for me over the years. I was thinking the other day about how a pastor can measure his effectiveness. It is really very simple as he looks at the buildings that God allows him to build and the attendance that the Lord allows him to attain. However, for an evangelist there really is no way to measure your effectiveness by using those means. The only way that I know of that an evangelist can measure his effectiveness is by the pulpits that he is allowed to preach in and by the pastors who invest their confidence in him. If that be the case, then I certainly have attained some measure of success in light of the fact that I am allowed into churches like yours. Brother Chappell, you are one of the most amazing an unusual young men that I have ever known. I am so thrilled at what I see happening at the Lancaster Baptist Church. Brother Paul, I was stunned to see the crowd that was in church on a Sunday evening. To think that you had well over 400 is just an unbelievable accomplishment in the length of time that God has had you in Lancaster as the pastor of the church.

Brother Chappell, I am so proud to be your friend. I tell you often, but I want you to know it from the depths of my heart that I love you very much. I am so honored that you allowed me an occasion to come and have a part in the ministry that God has given to you at Lancaster.

The love gift that you and your church gave to me was an amazing amount of money. I could not believe it when I saw the checks. My heart is so filled with gratitude and appreciation. Please express my love and my thanks to your people. Remember us in your prayers. Thank you again for your love and your kindness.

Sincerely,

E. W. Davis
Evangelist

EWD:pgc

Dr. Jack A. Trieber, Pastor        Zip Code 95054        Telephone 408/988-8881

TENNESSEE TEMPLE UNIVERSITY

6/19

Dear Brother Chappell,

Thank you for your kind letter which I have just received.

I am honored to have been asked to speak for your Leadership Conference next July 11-13. I am also a bit awed by the responsibility, but if the Lord spares me until then I will try to be with you.

It was good to have had those few minutes together at B.I.M.I. I will look forward to seeing you at the Dec. 7-8 meeting.

God bless you richly
J.R. Faulkner

J.R. Faulkner

1815 UNION AVENUE • CHATTANOOGA, TENNESSEE 37404 • 615/493-4100
HOME 423/892-3621 OFF. 423/493-4113

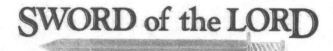

**SWORD of the LORD**

Dr. Curtis Hutson
President and Editor

Post Office Box 1099
Murfreesboro, TN 37133

May 13, 1991

Pastor Paul Chappell
Lancaster Baptist Church
304 West Lancaster Blvd.
Lancaster, CA 93534

Dear Paul:

I enjoyed being with you and the good people there at Lancaster
Baptist Church for your annual big day. I can hardly believe
the many hours that your people put in, preparing for this big
Sunday--30,000 visits is almost unbelievable! But it certainly
paid off. If only one soul had been saved, it would have been
worth all your efforts multiplied ten times and more; but over
200 salvation decisions is something to shout about!

Paul, I appreciate the nice motel room, the delicious fruit
basket, and the opportunity to get SWORD subscriptions. I do
want THE SWORD OF THE LORD to be a blessing to you and your
people. Our ministry is a ministry to Christians and local
churches. I appreciate, too, the generous love offering and
the help with our expenses.

I hope you had a good day Monday with your father.

We had a good flight home. I didn't arrive in Nashville until
after 7:00 Monday evening.

Please do continue praying for us and our ministry here and
know that our prayers are for you. The Lord is using you in a
wonderful way, and I rejoice in every report of God's blessings
upon your ministry.

Very sincerely,

Curtis Hutson

CH:sp

"America's Foremost Revival Publication"

# SWORD of the LORD

Dr. Curtis Hutson
President and Editor

Post Office Box 1099
Murfreesboro, TN 37133

September 9, 1994


Pastor Paul Chappell
Lancaster Baptist Church
4020 East Lancaster Blvd.
Lancaster, CA 93535

Dear Paul:

I was glad to hear about your "Family Pride Day" at Lancaster
Baptist Church. I was happy to see that you kept soul winning
your main business and had 25 people saved on that special day!

Paul, I cannot tell you how proud I am of you and the great
work you are doing there on the West Coast. I recommended to
Clarence Sexton that he have you for a conference, and I'm glad
you two got acquainted.

I regret so very much that I could not be there for the Sword
Conference. Only God knows how much I wanted to be a part of
that meeting!

Every letter from you is like a breath of fresh air from the
West Coast. It looks to me like God has raised up you, Jack
Trieber, and maybe some others whom I do not know about to hold
the banner high on that side of the country.

I don't know how much longer I have for this world. I just
came home from a 10-day unexpected visit to the hospital, and
the doctor does not hold out any hope for me. However, life
and death are in the hands of the Lord, not medical science.
It may please the Lord to bring about a miracle and raise me
up, but I'm not fussy about that. I want His will done in my
life whether it be living or dying--He is the Boss! And if
I could, I wouldn't have it any other way. He is too wise to
be mistaken.

I challenge you to take your place in the long line of independent, fundamental Baptists who have stood for separation and soul
winning (and I speak now especially of ecclesiastical separation)
and to hold that banner high until Jesus comes or God calls you
Home.


"America's Foremost Revival Publication"

Pastor Paul Chappell
September 9, 1994
Page 2

Thanks for the sermon you sent on tape. I'll have it transcribed and, the Lord willing, I'll read it for possible use in the SWORD. In the meantime, please send us several sermons that you have preached recently, sermons that you feel were a special blessing to your people or that God used in a special way. I'd like to run some of your sermons in the SWORD OF THE LORD. And we need them here so the girls can take them off tape. We'll edit them ourselves.

Now, remember that I'm asking for them. I feel it is of the Lord. I've instructed John Reynolds, in case something happens to me, to use some of your sermons in the paper. I love you very much. Please give my love to the precious people there at Lancaster Baptist Church, and I thank God for our fond memories and that He allowed me to be there several times and witness the growth and blessings of God upon that place.

Keep your chin up and your knees down and don't ever quit!

With my love, and prayers,

Curtis Hutson

CH:sp

## First Baptist Church of Hammond

### In Indiana

Five Twenty-Three Sibley Street
P.O. Box 6448

April 9, 1991

Pastor Paul Chappell
Lancaster Baptist Church
304 W. Lancaster Boulevard
Lancaster, California 93534

Dear Brother Chappell:

Though you are not one of my preacher boys from First Baptist Church, somehow I feel as though you are. Though you are not one of our Hyles-Anderson College graduates, I somehow feel that you are. When I think of you, I think of you as one of my boys and feel the same type pride that I feel when I think of those young men who have gone out from our ministry here.

Through the years I have seen young men rise on the scene who were a cut above the others. This is the way I have watched you through these years.

May I congratulate you, your family and your people as you share this occasion together. You have a wonderful past and an even greater future. God has used you miraculously, and is going to use you even more greatly.

Dr. Myron Cedarholm once said that there are very, very few men who start in the ministry at a young age who stay true to their separatist Baptist position all the way to old age. I am confident that you will be one of those men.

God bless you. I love you, and I am proud of you.

Sincerely,

Jack Hyles

JH:mb

Jack Hyles, Pastor       Zip Code 46325       219-932-0711

## Grace Baptist Church
### Dr. Bob Kelley, Pastor
*416 Denham Avenue*
*West Columbia, South Carolina 29169*
*Phone: 803-794-8237*
*Fax: 803-739-1204*

*"And there they preached the Gospel." Acts 14:7*

*AWANA Ministry*

*Bus Ministry*

*Day Care Ministry*

*Deaf Ministry*

*Faith Missions*

*Ft. Jackson*

*Grace Bible Studies*

*Grace Christian School*

*Hispanic*

*Junior Church*

*Music Ministry*

*Senior Saints Ministry*

*Tape Ministry*

*Youth Ministry*

May 29, 2001

Dr. Paul Chappell
Pastor of Lancaster Baptist Church
and President of West Coast Baptist Coast
4020 East Lancaster Blvd.
Lancaster, CA 93535

Dear Dr. Paul,

Please let me express my deepest thanks for the wonderful opportunity to be at West Coast Baptist College. What a challenge to me. I believe God has raised you up to be a leader of fundamentalism in our day. You are proving it can still be done without changing methods or doctrines. Amen!

Praise the Lord for the fifty-two graduates. I trust the Lord will bless them greatly.

Also, let me say thank you for the kind and generous way you treated me and my visit. Bro. Ruppert and Bro. Rasmussen were both genuine blessings. Thank them for me. I am sending three tapes of our daughters singing. I wanted all three of you to have one. Amen!

Sincerely in Christ,

Dr. Bob Kelley
Pastor

*Home of Grace Christian School*
*"Delightfully Different"*
*803-794-8996*

# Mark Lawrence

Pastor, Mrs Chappell, and Emily,

I got a foretaste of Heaven yesterday. I cannot put words to my gratitude for all that God has done.

You have been the single greatest blessing to ever come into my life besides Jesus and my family. Thank you for your patience, love and friendship.

Whatever the Lord has in the future, I can look forward to — He has already shown me more love than I can comprehend. Thank you for being the instruments of it

I love you  Bro Lawrence

# Mark Lawrence

Pastor,

I have been praying for you this morning, that you would stay, that you would live long, that you would keep preaching just as strong as ever, that you would sense the presence of the Lord even more as the Devil fights, and that God continues to give you strength and wisdom.

You have been used of God so much in my life, and in the life of my family — thank you for being ~~joyfully~~ obedient.

Have a great day, love

P.S. you should get a special surprise this week from Oregon! Merry Christmas
Bro. Mark

# Mark Lawrence

Pastor,

I was thinking of you and wanted you to know. I pray constantly for you, your church, and lately much for your college.

I know the pressure must be intense — God only knows, but thank you for your faithfulness.

I look forward to the time when I can see you in a few days.

God has surely been blessing here, pray for stamina as we work _til Jesus comes_.

Say hello to your wonderful wife and family. We love you all.

Bro AL

# Mark Lawrence

Pastor,

Just a note to tell you I was praying for you this week during the conference. Diane said it was great (awsome was the word she used).

This is kind of a crazier summer than usual, they probally won't get much better as everyone thinks they should not get married unless it is over 100°. I've tried always to teach February weddings (among other sensible things)

Anyway I do still love you and hope we can get a few moments 24th at this month. Bro Mark

# Mark Lawrence

Pastor,

What a blessing you were to me, my wife, and Laura during our visit. I thank God for you and your friendship, and I hope your church knows how much I love and appreciate them as well. It is hard to put into words how much you and your staff and church family mean to Diane and I.

We have been praying for you and your family many times a day, the girls have been praying with us for your health and stamina, and protection during these last days.

Thank you for your hard work - with the tree project on top of everything else, you have been a blessing to us so many times and I hope we were a help and not a hindrance with the trees. It sure was fun! We love you,

Mark & Diane Lawrence

*Providence*
**Baptist Church**                                    Pastor Mark Lawrence

Corner of Front & Main • Prairie City OR 97869                    1•541• 820•4757

Pastor Chappell,

Thank you for your letters, calls and especially prayers. This year has been a whirl and only shows how brief our time here is! So much has happened, yet always God gets the glory!

By the time you read this we will be on our way to see you, but I want you to know how much I love and appreciate you. I am praying for you, your family, and your church.

Your friend

*" Holding Forth the Word "*.... *Phil. 2:16*

282

810/334-0961

**Midwestern**

**BAPTIST COLLEGE &
BAPTIST BIBLE SEMINARY**
825 Golf Drive
Pontiac, Michigan 48341

July 22, 1998

Lancaster Baptist Church,
Dr. Paul Chappell
4020 E. Lancaster Blvd.
Lancaster, CA 93535

Dear Brother Paul,

Thank you for the invitation to speak at your Spiritual Leadership Conference in July of 1999. I would be honored to accept.

If it is possible, I would prefer to speak Monday night and Tuesday morning on Monday, July 12th and Tuesday, July 13th. Also I would prefer to be the first speaker at these two services. You have been so helpful to me in the past and I appreciate it. I would also like for you to make the flight arrangements, non-stop from Detroit to California and let them know I would need a shuttle or wheel chair for going through the terminal as I cannot walk great distances now with my legs affecting me so badly.

Please contact my secretary, Margo Higginbotham with the arrangements and if you have any questions.

I pray for you and your great ministry that God will bless all you do. My wife and I are well. We just returned from a much needed rest in Florida. God is on the throne and He will meet all your needs, He has been so good to us. Thank you for being a faithful friend.

In Christ,

Tom Malone Sr.

Dr. Tom Malone Sr.,
President

Dr. Tom Malone, Sr. - President

A    COLLEGE    OF    DISTINCTION:    SINCE    1953

LEE ROBERSON CENTER

OFFICE OF THE CHANCELLOR

**TENNESSEE TEMPLE**
*University*
*Distinctively Christian*
1815 UNION AVENUE
CHATTANOOGA, TENNESSEE 37404
TELEPHONE 615/493-4115

October 10, 1990

Rev. Paul W. Chappell
Lancaster Baptist Church
304 West Lancaster Boulevard
Lancaster, CA   93534

Dear Brother Chappell:

I am leaving in a few moments for a meeting in Detroit, Michigan, and for other meetings throughout the nation.  This morning I thought of you and prayed for you and for your great ministry in California! I do rejoice in all that you are doing and pray that God will keep on blessing and guiding you.

It is my prayer that some day I will be able to visit with you and your people.  Be assured of my prayers for you and for your church and for your family.

Sincerely,

Lee Roberson
Chancellor

LR:gs

LEE ROBERSON CENTER

OFFICE OF THE CHANCELLOR

**TENNESSEE TEMPLE**
*University*
*Distinctively Christian*
1815 UNION AVENUE
CHATTANOOGA, TENNESSEE 37404
TELEPHONE 615/493-4115

June 14, 1991

Rev. Paul W. Chappell
Lancaster Baptist Church
304 West Lancaster Boulevard
Lancaster, CA 93534

Dear Brother Chappell:

We arrived home last evening and I am beginning my work today by writing to you.

Thank you for every kindness extended to me and my wife during our three days with you and your people! We enjoyed all of our time with you.

Thank you for planning the services so carefully. The Sunday School meetings, the choir, and, yes, every part of your work, showed concern and planning.

You have done a mighty work in Lancaster in the last five years! If the Lord tarries, I believe there are great and mighty things ahead for you and for your people. I can visualize the new church building and the expansion of all of your ministry.

Thank you for the generous offering given to us! This will be used in the work of our Saviour.

Our prayers will be for you and your wife and your children! The Lord has given you a wonderful family.

I shall be praying for the continued growth of your ministry and for the reaching of definite goals in attendance and in the winning of souls.

Thank you again for every kindness to us. We are deeply grateful.

Sincerely,

Lee Roberson
Chancellor

LR:gs

STUDENT SERVICES BUILDING
OFFICE OF THE CHANCELLOR

**TENNESSEE TEMPLE**
*University*
*Distinctively Christian*

1815 UNION AVENUE
CHATTANOOGA, TENNESSEE 37404
TELEPHONE 615/698-6021

July 12, 1996

Dr. Paul Chappell
Lancaster Baptist Church
4020 East Lancaster Boulevard
Lancaster, CA  93535

Dear Brother Chappell:

It is Friday morning and I am back in Chattanooga.

What a joy to be with you and your people in the services this week!  The Lord has given you an amazing and wonderful church.  Your people are loyal, enthusiastic, and zealous in the winning of souls.

They love you, respect you, and are eager to follow your leadership.  I did not hear one single word of discord during my time with you.  The people are happy and rejoicing in all that is taking place.

Thank you for the generous offering given to us.  This will be used in the work of our Saviour.

My prayers will continue for you, your wife, and your children.  I will be praying for the ongoing of your church. I am sure that you will soon be starting a new building.  You need additional space.

May God's richest blessings be on you.

Sincerely

Lee Roberson
Chancellor

LR:gs
P.S.  If any of my books were not sold, please feel free to
      ship them back to us.

*LEE ROBERSON, D. D., LL. D., Founder-Chancellor*

LEE ROBERSON CENTER

OFFICE OF THE CHANCELLOR

**TENNESSEE TEMPLE**
*University*
*Distinctively Christian*

1815 UNION AVENUE
CHATTANOOGA, TENNESSEE 37404
TELEPHONE 423/493-4118

**October 6, 2004**

Dr. Paul Chappell
**Lancaster Baptist Church**
**4020 East Lancaster Boulevard**
Lancaster, CA 93535

**Dear Brother Chappell:**

Thank you for your letter received a few days ago.

I thank the Lord for you and for your faithful ministry. I am glad to hear that your work is growing and many are being saved and baptized.

Whenever you see souls being saved and the stirring of the hearts of people, others will criticize. Preachers are especially guilty of criticizing other preachers who are doing a good job.

If your work is succeeding, people are coming to Christ, and the church is growing in the work of God, I would keep pressing on, ignore the criticism, and follow the leadership of the Lord.

May God's richest blessings be on you and all of your work.

Sincerely,

Lee Roberson
Chancellor

LR:gs

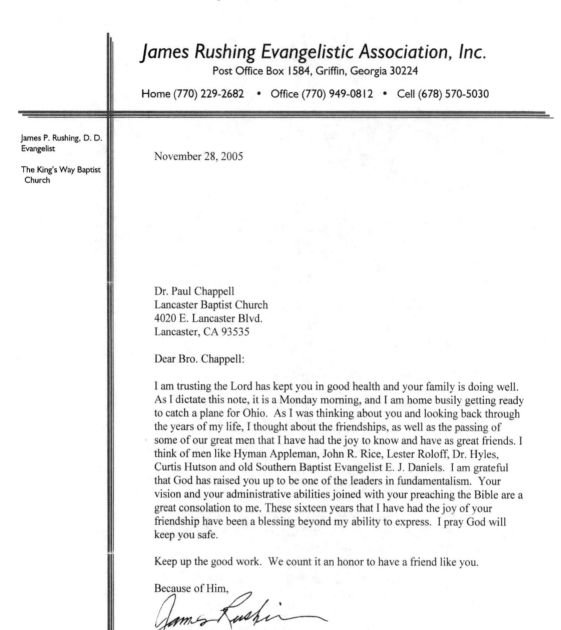

## James Rushing Evangelistic Association, Inc.
Post Office Box 1584, Griffin, Georgia 30224

Home (770) 229-2682 • Office (770) 949-0812 • Cell (678) 570-5030

James P. Rushing, D. D.
Evangelist

The King's Way Baptist
Church

November 28, 2005

Dr. Paul Chappell
Lancaster Baptist Church
4020 E. Lancaster Blvd.
Lancaster, CA 93535

Dear Bro. Chappell:

I am trusting the Lord has kept you in good health and your family is doing well. As I dictate this note, it is a Monday morning, and I am home busily getting ready to catch a plane for Ohio. As I was thinking about you and looking back through the years of my life, I thought about the friendships, as well as the passing of some of our great men that I have had the joy to know and have as great friends. I think of men like Hyman Appleman, John R. Rice, Lester Roloff, Dr. Hyles, Curtis Hutson and old Southern Baptist Evangelist E. J. Daniels. I am grateful that God has raised you up to be one of the leaders in fundamentalism. Your vision and your administrative abilities joined with your preaching the Bible are a great consolation to me. These sixteen years that I have had the joy of your friendship have been a blessing beyond my ability to express. I pray God will keep you safe.

Keep up the good work. We count it an honor to have a friend like you.

Because of Him,

James Rushing

James Rushing

JR:bjr

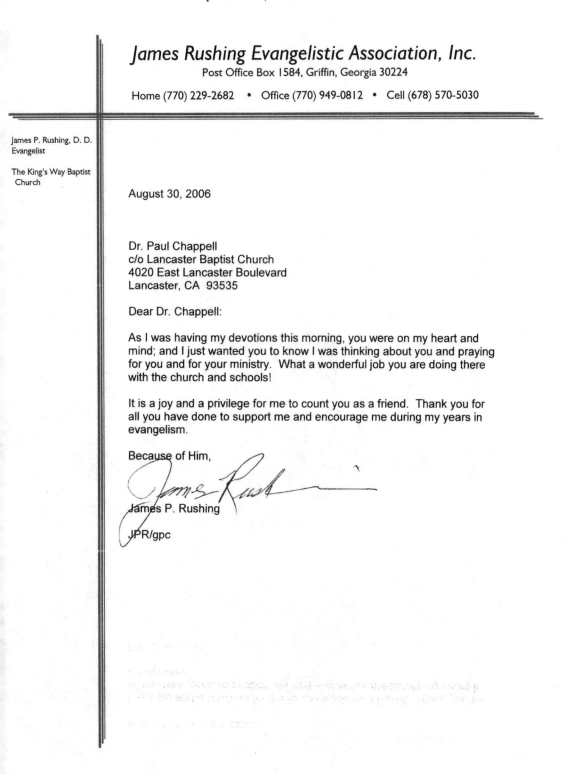

# James Rushing Evangelistic Association, Inc.

Post Office Box 1584, Griffin, Georgia 30224

Home (770) 229-2682 • Office (770) 949-0812 • Cell (678) 570-5030

James P. Rushing, D. D.
Evangelist

The King's Way Baptist
Church

August 30, 2006

Dr. Paul Chappell
c/o Lancaster Baptist Church
4020 East Lancaster Boulevard
Lancaster, CA 93535

Dear Dr. Chappell:

As I was having my devotions this morning, you were on my heart and mind; and I just wanted you to know I was thinking about you and praying for you and for your ministry. What a wonderful job you are doing there with the church and schools!

It is a joy and a privilege for me to count you as a friend. Thank you for all you have done to support me and encourage me during my years in evangelism.

Because of Him,

James P. Rushing

JPR/gpc

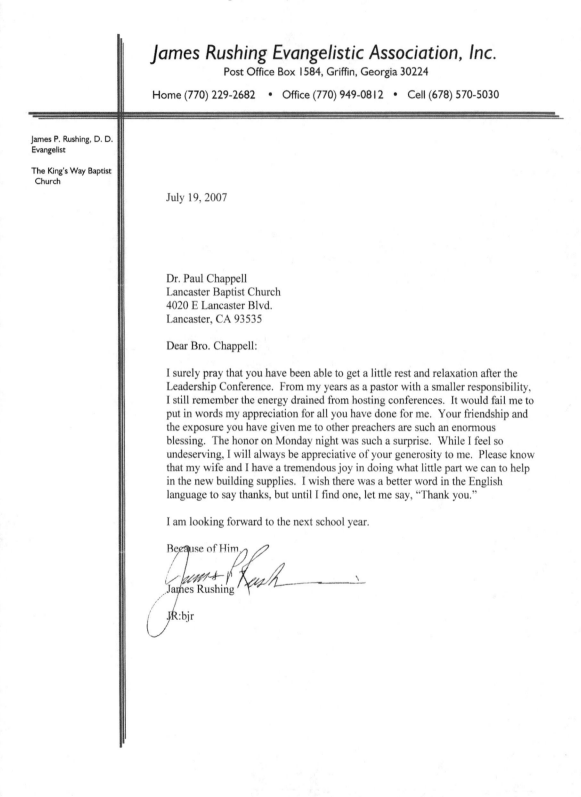

## James Rushing Evangelistic Association, Inc.

Post Office Box 1584, Griffin, Georgia 30224

Home (770) 229-2682  •  Office (770) 949-0812  •  Cell (678) 570-5030

James P. Rushing, D. D.
Evangelist

The King's Way Baptist
 Church

July 19, 2007


Dr. Paul Chappell
Lancaster Baptist Church
4020 E Lancaster Blvd.
Lancaster, CA 93535

Dear Bro. Chappell:

I surely pray that you have been able to get a little rest and relaxation after the
Leadership Conference. From my years as a pastor with a smaller responsibility,
I still remember the energy drained from hosting conferences. It would fail me to
put in words my appreciation for all you have done for me. Your friendship and
the exposure you have given me to other preachers are such an enormous
blessing. The honor on Monday night was such a surprise. While I feel so
undeserving, I will always be appreciative of your generosity to me. Please know
that my wife and I have a tremendous joy in doing what little part we can to help
in the new building supplies. I wish there was a better word in the English
language to say thanks, but until I find one, let me say, "Thank you."

I am looking forward to the next school year.

Because of Him

James Rushing

JR:bjr

November 4, 1996

Viola Walden,
*Sword of the Lord*
224 Bridge Avenue
Murfreesboro, TN 37412

Dear Viola,

This past Friday I received the edited manuscript from my TEAM soul winning book which we have been revising. It was interesting to read your comments and revisions.

I want you to know how much I appreciate you taking the time out of your busy schedule to help us with this project. Our editting lady, Amy Cox, plans on studying your comments to learn from them.

The Lord has certainly used you there at the *Sword* to be a blessing to thousands of readers. Thank you for your ministry there, and thank you again for your willingness to be a help to us. Have a great day!

Sincerely in Christ,

Dr. Paul Chappell
Pastor

*Dr. Chappell, how the public (who does not know you), & how the Church hears you -- these are two different groups. We want to present the written message to well represent you.*

*(over)*

*"1996 . . . He is Able"*

Yours are no different than Dr. Rice's were, or Hyles' as spoken, or Dr. Roberson's — he wanted me to always read his before even if another printed did his books. they went to press, + Correct, So don't feel that we are Critical. This is true of any spoken message.

If I can help you with your books (I studied this in Journalism), please let me. I'm always looking for way to help preachers especially. I learned this from my great boss, Dr. Rice!

Best greetings.

Viola

11/6/96

Dear Dr. Chappell:

The whole office is envious! Dr. Byers came through, followed by a crowd, wanting to know who was getting such lovely flowers! He was the delivery boy. Thank you! Thank you! But you didn't need to do that. It was my joy to help. Gratefully,

Viola

Viola Walden

# PROFESSIONAL
# ACQUAINTANCES

FRANKLIN GRAHAM
P. O. Box 3000, Boone, N. C. 28607

October 30, 2001

Dr. Paul Chappell
Lancaster Baptist Church
4020 Lancaster Boulevard
Lancaster, CA 93535

Dear Dr. Chappell:

Thank you for your letter of October 22 concerning the Robert Schuller interview with my father a few years ago. I appreciate your concern and the fact that you would write for clarification.

I am quite aware of the incident that you mentioned; and from all indications Dr. Schuller did lead my father down an uncertain path. Through the editing process of the interview, it sounded like my father was saying that there are many ways to Heaven. This, of course, is not true. My father and I both believe that the only way to Heaven is through the shed blood of God's Son, the Lord Jesus Christ.

My father is 83 years old and we have been encouraging him not to do interviews. His hearing is not what it used to be; and for the past several years, he has been medicated for Parkinson's disease. He had many side effects from this medication, further complicating his problems. Last year the doctors discovered that he had normal pressure hydrocephalus (a buildup of spinal fluid in the brain). Since that time, they have inserted two shunts to relieve the pressure. I am happy to say that he is doing much better. In fact, he's doing remarkably well. I know that he would appreciate your prayers.

Thank you again for writing. May God bless you in your ministry.

Sincerely,

Franklin Graham

FG/jd

**John C. Maxwell**
Founder

**Dick Peterson**
President

May 15, 1995

Pastor Paul Chappell
Lancaster Baptist Church
4020 East Lancaster Blvd.
Lancaster, CA 93535

Dear Paul:

I enjoyed our recent time together. I want to encourage you to attend one of my leadership conferences. I believe it would help give further direction and insight to you and your ministry. I will also make sure that you receive information on the mentoring program that I and my team at INJOY are developing.

Please accept as my gift the enclosed materials. Today I prayed for you, your family, and your ministry.

Your friend,

John C. Maxwell

JCM:lje

1530 Jamacha Road, Suite D • El Cajon, California 92019 • 619-444-8400 • 1-800-333-6506 • FAX 619-444-9033

**Bellevue**
Baptist Church

*A Family of Friends*

OFFICE OF THE PASTOR

2000 Appling Road

Cordova, Tennessee 38016

(901) 347-2000

Dr. Adrian Rogers, Pastor

October 13, 2004

Dr. Paul Chappell
Lancaster Baptist Church
4020 E. Lancaster Blvd.
Lancaster, CA 93535

Dear Brother Paul:

Thank you for the book. I have not yet gone through it, but just from the outside it looks great.

I thank God for His mighty hand upon your church.

In Jesus' name,

Adrian Rogers

lg

OFFICE OF THE PRESIDENT

January 23, 2001

Dr. and Mrs. Paul Chappell
Lancaster Baptist Church
4020 East Lancaster Blvd.
Lancaster, CA 93535

Dear Paul and Terrie:

Thank you for your letter dated January 10. Congratulations on twenty years of marriage! You are setting a wonderful example for your flock.

I appreciate your candor in suggesting that grace has been used as a license, or excuse, for some taking liberties. Obviously, I have written extensively on the subject. I am continually amazed at the power and fragile nature of God's offer of unmerited favor. Grace is an explosive gift from God. Can it be abused? Of course. Has it been embraced by people wanting a dumping ground for disobedience? You bet. Yet, God still offers grace on a daily basis, knowing it may be, and often is, overlooked, or worse, abused. That's why it's so amazing.

Thank you, Paul and Terrie, for being careful shepherds through the years. Stay at it!

With great hope,

Charles R. Swindoll
President

CRS:ps

3909 SWISS AVENUE • DALLAS, TEXAS 75204 • 214-824-3094 • 800-992-0998 • www.dts.edu

**Panic Note!**

from the desk of

*C. Sumner Wemp*

Dear Paul,

Bless you. What a joy to meet you & hear you after hearing so much about you from the Teis's especially & of course hearing from all over how God has used you to build a great church & a great school, you run the well. You love the Jesus & people

"We want to your house yesterday, but we couldn't find you."

just stand out, I rejoice in the way God is using you.

I felt the conference was unusually good. My cup got filled.

May the dear Lord keep His hand upon you & your school.

I love you dear brother

all because of Calvary

Sumner & Celeste

1 Pet 3:2

# Index

# Part 2—25 Years of Correspondence

West Coast Baptist College Library

10000000006034